LAKSHMI

The Goddess of Wealth and Fortune

An Introduction

To the gods
and to the demons
who dance in my dreams
And to my father,
Late Shri Prafulla Kumar Pattanaik

Lakshmi, the goddess of wealth and
fortune; wood carving from Kerala

LAKSHMI

The Goddess of Wealth and Fortune

An Introduction

Devdutt Pattanaik

Vakils, Feffer and Simons Private Ltd.
Hague Building, 9, Sprott Road, Ballard Estate,
Mumbai 400 001. India

First printing 2003

Price Rs. 295/-

Published by Bimal Mehta
for Vakils, Feffer and Simons Private Ltd.
Hague Building, 9, Sprott Road, Ballard Estate
Mumbai 400 001. India

Printed by Arun K. Mehta at Vakil & Sons Private Ltd.
Industry Manor, Appasaheb Marathe Marg
Worli, Mumbai 400 025. India

ISBN 81-87111-58-5

Contents

Acknowledgements

This book would not have been possible without the support, insight and love of those mentioned below:

My parents, who were always puzzled by my uncanny interest in mythology and my sisters, Seema and Shami, who have struggled with my unconventional ways

Arunbhai, for believing that there is value in recording the beliefs of our ancestors for our children and our children's children

Giri and Shailaja, David and Charmayne for those wonderful conversations

Parag, for providing me the platform to talk on the subject

Nimu, for challenging my views on worldliness

Manohar and Nagendra for helping me compile images

Rajeshree, for colouring all my illlustrations and her many suggestions to enhance the quality of text and layout

Sudhakar Tawade and everyone at Vakils, for their dedicated contribution to the project

My *shakti*, my life, my world, sometimes manifesting as the alluring Lakshmi and sometimes as the enlightening Saraswati

Thank You.

About this book

What is the purpose of life? The answer according to the Veda is fourfold: *dharma, artha, kama* and *moksha*, which means righteous conduct, economic activity, pleasurable pursuit and spiritual practice.

Economic activity has been given great importance in the Hindu scheme of things. It is second only to *dharma*, that ensures social stability. With social stability comes prosperity and with prosperity comes pleasure.
To drive this idea home, ancient seers visualised a goddess called Lakshmi. She embodied the principle of *artha*. She sat at the feet of Vishnu who embodied the principle of *dharma*. Her son was Manmatha who embodied the principle of *kama*.

Lakshmi is one of the most popular Hindu goddesses. Her stories, symbols and rituals are widespread and they contain the Hindu understanding of wealth. Unfortunately, these were passed down orally within the household tradition. They were neither compiled nor commented upon in a single scripture. As a result there is great misunderstanding on how Hindus regard wealth. Some believe that Hindus look down upon wealth. This belief stems from the popularity of Indian monastic philosophies like yoga and Vedanta. Others believe that Hindus think wealth is evil. This belief is based on the association of Lakshmi with *asura*s and *rakshasa*s, the 'demons' of Hinduism. An examination of the mythology of Lakshmi helps us appreciate that none of this is true. Not only did Hindus revere Lakshmi as the foundation of things material, they also believed she was vital to all things spiritual. Only by truly appreciating the nature of Lakshmi can one hope for *moksha*, release from the cycle of rebirths.

A study of Lakshmi throws light on the fact that there is no concept of evil in Hinduism. Evil is a Judeo-Christian-Islamic concept to explain negative acts that are unholy, inexplicable and unredeemable. In the Hindu scheme of things, where everything is governed by the law of *karma*, all events are essentially reactions. Nothing is spontaneous. Everything is a manifestation of God.

The reason why Lakshmi is closely associated with *asura*s and *rakshasa*s has nothing to do with evil. It has everything to do with the movement of wealth between realms above the ground and below, between wild nature and domesticated culture.

Although eternal enemies of gods and humans, neither the *asura* nor the *rakshasa* is evil. *Asura*s are subterranean forces that have the power to regenerate wealth, hence necessary components of the cosmos (without their help, the *deva*s cannot churn Lakshmi out of the ocean of milk). However, since they hoard this regenerated wealth, they have to be killed by the gods who release and redistribute wealth. *Rakshasa*s are barbarians who follow the law of the jungle: might is right. They do not share wealth with the weak and do not respect the rights of others as demonstrated by the *rakshasa*-king Ravana when he abducted Rama's wife Sita. Rama has to kill Ravana and release Sita in order to establish the law of civilisation: the weak have rights and the strong have duties. *Asura*s and *rakshasa*s are demons, not because they are evil, but because they hoard and plunder wealth, hindering the normal flow of wealth.

Since wealth has to flow, Lakshmi is given the rather unflattering title of Chanchala — the restless one. She never stays with demons for long. She does not stay with the gods either. Even Indra, king of *deva*s, loses the grace of Lakshmi when he overindulges with wine and women at the cost of his duty, earning the ire of sages. Thus the cycle of life-bestowing wealth — represented by the never-ending battles of the gods and demons known as *deva-asura-sangrama* — continues with its alternating successes and failures.

Having understood the nature of wealth, ancient gurus prescribed the following formula to become rich: do not obstruct the flow of wealth, do not hoard, do not plunder, simply ensure wealth flows continuously in the desired direction. This prescription was given ritual form by the practice of painting *Shri-pada*, Lakshmi's footprint, on the threshold of the house pointing inwards.

Such insight into the traditional understanding of wealth can be gathered from the stories, symbols and rituals of Lakshmi. This book is an attempt to compile and understand this fascinating mythology of Lakshmi in a systematic manner. It is not an in-depth study, but simply an introduction for the lay reader. For those seeking a deeper insight there is a select bibliography at the end of the book. It is hoped that the book is comprehensive, clear, cohesive and concise enough to make Lakshmi walk in the desired direction — into all our lives.

— **Devdutt Pattanaik**

Diwali, 2003

Within infinite myths lies the Eternal Truth.
Who sees it all?
Varuna has but a thousand eyes,
Indra has a hundred,
And I, only two.

Lakshmi, the golden goddess of
auspiciousness, affluence and abundance;
Patta painting from Orissa.

The Lakshmi Heritage

Draped in red saree, bedecked with gold ornaments, seated on a lotus, pot in hand, flanked by white elephants, the image of Lakshmi adorns most Hindu homes and business establishments.

Lakshmi is goddess of wealth, fortune, power, luxury, beauty, fertility, and auspiciousness. She holds the promise of material fulfilment and contentment. She is described as restless, whimsical yet maternal, with her arms raised to bless and to grant. For centuries Hindus have invoked her thus:

> Beautiful goddess seated on a chariot,
> Delighted by songs on lustful elephants,
> Bedecked with lotuses, pearls and gems,
> Lustrous as fire, radiant as gold,
> Resplendent as the sun, calm as the moon,
> Mistress of cows and horses —
> Take away poverty and misfortune
> Bring joy, riches, harvest and children.

The world may have changed, but the thirst for material comfort continues to form the core of most human aspirations.

Shri — the Sacred Name

The popularity of Lakshmi can be gauged by the fact that her sacred name — Shri. Shri is written atop most documents and spoken before addressing a god, a teacher, a holy man or any revered individual. The word evokes amongst other things:

- Grace
- Affluence
- Abundance
- Auspiciousness
- Authority

When the word is spoken or written, an aura of holiness is established. Whatever follows the word is imbued with divine blessing.

Married men and women are addressed as Shriman and Shrimati as they have Lakshmi's blessings to harness the wealth of the world to support family and sustain society. Ascetics are not addressed as Shriman as they have renounced worldly riches; unmarried men and women are not addressed as Shriman and Shrimati as they are still in preparation for the householder's life.

Just as the word 'aum' is associated with the mystical side of life, the word 'shri' is associated with the material side of existence.

Chapter I

Shri is the sacred sound of cosmic auspiciousness and abundance since Vedic times.

Lakshmi, the goddess of prosperity; modern calendar art.

Ancient Romans had their own form of Lakshmi known as Demeter, the corn-goddess or Magna Mater, the great mother of the cosmos.

In Jain tradition, Lakshmi and her symbols such as elephant, cow, pot, throne, and gems appeared in the dreams of women who were about to give birth to holy men; 14th century tapestry from Gujarat.

Widespread Appeal

The practice of personifying the beauty and bounty of earth as a goddess was prevalent in all ancient cultures. The Greeks had **Core**, the corn-goddess, who was known to Romans as **Demeter**. The Egyptians had **Isis**, Sumerians had **Innana**, Babylonians had **Ishtar**, Persians had **Anahita** and Vikings had **Freia**. **Shri-Lakshmi** is the Hindu form of the timeless mother-goddess who nurtures and nourishes all life.

In India, not only Hindus but also Buddhists and Jains adore Lakshmi. Buddhism and Jainism are primarily monastic orders that turned away from Vedic rituals and Brahmanical dogmas about 2500 years ago. They, however, could not abandon this delightful goddess.

In the Buddhist *Jataka*s, there are tales of men and women who request the goddess Lakshmi to drive away the goddess of misfortune, Kalakanni. Images of Kubera, the pot-bellied *yaksha*-king and treasurer of the gods, who is closely associated with Lakshmi, adorn most Buddhist shrines.

In holy Jain texts, it is said when an exalted soul like a *Tirthankara* is about to be born his mother dreams of many auspicious things including the goddess Shri.

Symbols of wealth and royal power commonly associated with Lakshmi are auspicious to both Buddhists and Jains. These include: the pot, a pile of gems, a throne, a flywhisk, a conch, a fish, a parasol, *naga*s, *yaksha*s, a footstool, a horse, an elephant, a cow, and the wish-fulfilling tree.

An Ancient Goddess

Shri-Lakshmi has a long history testified by the fact that her first hymn, the *Shri Shukta*, was added to the Rig Veda, the oldest and most revered of Hindu scriptures, somewhere between 1000 and 500 BC.

Considering her popularity amongst Buddhists and Jains, it has been proposed that her worship may predate the Vedic culture and may have developed independently before she was brought into the Vedic, Buddhist and Jain folds.

Scholars are of the view that initially the words Shri and Lakshmi referred to anything that was auspicious or brought good luck or bestowed riches and power. Later the two words were personified into two goddesses who eventually merged. Thus, Shri-Lakshmi came into being.

Fragmentary verses in the *Shatapatha Brahmana*, written not long after the *Veda*s, talks of the birth of Lakshmi from the mouth of Prajapati to provide the inhabitants of the cosmos food, clothing, shelter, and all things that make life more comfortable. She also offered wisdom, strength, beauty, luck, sovereignty and splendour — the good things in life.

Stories of Lakshmi first appeared in the epics *Ramayana* and *Mahabharta*, that were composed between 300 BC and 300 AD, a period that witnessed the waning popularity of Vedic gods and the rise of gods who offered *moksha* such as Shiva and Vishnu. Gods and demons

Hathor, the ancient Egyptian cow-goddess, was very similar to the Hindu Go-*mata*, the bovine form of Lakshmi.

In Persia, the goddess Anahita was the goddess of good fortune and charm, with characteristics similar to Lakshmi.

Ancient Indian silver coin from the Gupta period (300 AD) showing the image of Lakshmi.

fought over her and both strove to churn her out of the ocean of milk. As folk heroes such as Rama and Krishna were viewed as incarnations of Vishnu, their consorts Sita, Radha and Rukmini became increasingly identified with Lakshmi. In the *Harivamsa*, appendix to the *Mahabharata*, Manmatha, the god of love, lust and fertility, was described as her son.

The mythology of Lakshmi acquired full form in the *Purana*s, chronicles of gods, kings and sages that were compiled between 500 and 1500 AD. In them, the goddess came to be projected as one of the three primary forms of the supreme mother-goddess, the other two being Saraswati, the goddess of knowledge, and Kali or Durga, the goddess of power. Lakshmi was visualized both as an independent goddess and as Vishnu's consort, seated on his lap or at his feet.

Prithvi, the Vedic earth-goddess, became Bhoodevi in the *Purana*s and a manifestation of Lakshmi. In South India, the two goddesses were visualized as two different entities, standing on either side of Vishnu, Bhoodevi representing tangible wealth while Lakshmi or Shridevi representing intangible wealth. In North India, the two goddesses became one.

Images of Lakshmi started appearing around the third century BC in sculptures found in Kausambi, in North India, and on coins issued during the reign of the Gupta dynasty around the fourth century AD. She became a favourite of kings as more and more people believed she was the bestower of power, wealth and sovereignty. Separate shrines to Lakshmi within the precincts of Vishnu temples may have been built as early as the seventh century; such shrines were definitely in existence by the tenth century AD.

Popular 20th century image showing Lakshmi at the feet of Vishnu.

2000-year-old image of Lakshmi from a gateway of a Buddhist stupa at Bharhut indicating her popularity amongst non-Hindus too.

5

In Vedic times, Lakshmi was associated with the elephant-riding rain-god Indra (left), the crocodile-riding sea-god Varuna (centre) and the antelope-riding moon-god Soma (right); Mysore paintings.

Fickle and Independent

Nowadays, Hindus accept Lakshmi as the eternal consort of Vishnu, the preserver of the world. In her long history, however, the goddess has been associated with many other deities.

According to *Ramayana*, *Mahabharata* and *Purana*s, the goddess Lakshmi first lived with the demons before the gods acquired her. She graced *asura*s such as Hiranayaksha, Hiranakashipu, Prahalad, Virochana and Bali, *rakshasa*s such as Ravana and *yaksha*s such as Kubera before she adorned the court of Indra, king of *deva*s, the most renowned of Vedic gods. Cities of the *asura*s (Hiranyapura), *yaksha*s (Alakapuri), *rakshasa*s (Lanka) and *naga*s (Bhogavati) have all been described as cities of gold, Lakshmi's mineral manifestation.

Within the Vedic pantheon, Lakshmi was linked with many gods, especially those associated with water bodies: Indra, the rain-god (bestower of fresh water); Varuna, the sea-god (source of all water); Soma, the moon-god (waxer and waner of tides). Indra's wife Sachi was also known as Puloma, which is the name of an *asura*-woman suggesting entry of Lakshmi from the world of *asura*s into world of *deva*s.

As the Vedic gods waned into insignificance around the fifth century BC, two gods came to dominate the classical Hindu worldview: the world renouncing hermit-god Shiva and the world affirming warrior-god Vishnu. Lakshmi was briefly associated with Shiva before she became the faithful consort of Vishnu-Narayana, the ultimate refuge of man. With Vishnu, she was domesticated. No longer fleet footed, she sat demurely by his side, on his lap or at his feet.

The association with many gods has led to Lakshmi being viewed as fickle, restless and independent. Sociologists view the mythology of Lakshmi's fickleness as indicative of her cult's resistance to being assimilated with mainstream Hinduism. Even today there is tension between the mythology of Lakshmi as an independent goddess and her mythology as Vishnu's consort.

Philosophers choose to view the fickleness and independence of Lakshmi as an allegory for the restlessness of fortune. More often than not, there are no rational explanations for fortune and misfortune. Good times come without warning and leave as suddenly.

Shri Vaishnava Tradition

In the twelfth century AD, a new form of Vaishnavism called Shri-Vaishnavism evolved in South India. Like other Vaishnava orders, it visualized Vishnu as the embodiment of the supreme divine principle. However, this order was unique as it refused to acknowledge Vishnu independently. It insisted on the presence of Lakshmi beside him.

For Shri-Vaishnava scholars, such as Vedanta Deshika, Lakshmi is indispensable while approaching Vishnu. He represents righteousness; she represents compassion. She is like a mother intervening between a stern father (God) and an errant son (the devotee).

Maha-Lakshmi, the Great Goddess

In Tantrik texts, which were composed around the same time as the *Purana*s, Lakshmi acquired supreme importance. She was Maha-Lakshmi, the supreme goddess.

Vishnu, bearer of the conch, discus, lotus and mace, became popular in the post-Vedic age as the cosmic-king who institutes and maintains laws for natural and social order; Patta painting from Orissa.

Lakshmi's association with Vishnu confirmed her exalted status in Hinduism; North Indian miniature painting showing Lakshmi seated on Vishnu's left lap.

Maha-Lakshmi, the Tantrik form of Lakshmi, is less the goddess of wealth and more the supreme mother-goddess; painting from Orissa.

Lakshmi is often differentiated from Maha-Lakshmi. While the former is the consort of Vishnu and the goddess of wealth, Maha-Lakshmi is viewed as an autonomous entity, the supreme embodiment of the mother-goddess. When worshipped as Maha-Lakshmi, Lakshmi is not visualized as a beautiful goddess seated on a lotus, pot in hand, but like a virginal warrior-goddess riding a lion, much like Durga. This form of the goddess is especially popular in Maharashtra.

Ancient *Pancharatra* texts that adore Maha-Lakshmi consider her to be the root of all creation. In the beginning, they say, the cosmic soul — the unfathomable unmanifest Narayana — desired to create the cosmos. But he did not have the resources to do so. As he pondered over this problem, his dormant energy, his *shakti*, burst forth in a blinding light, manifesting as Maha-Lakshmi. Maha-Lakshmi placed the seed of divine desire in the palm of her hand and unleashed the dynamic forces of creation until the three worlds took shape and all forms of life came forth.

In the *Lakshmi Tantra*, the goddess says: "I am inherent in existence. I am the inciter, the potential that takes shape. I manifest myself. I occupy myself with activity and finally dissolve myself. I pervade all creations with vitality, will and consciousness. Like ghee that keeps a lamp burning, I lubricate the senses of living beings with the sap of my consciousness."

Lakshmi is the divine power that transforms dreams into reality. She is *prakriti*, the perfect creation: self-sustaining, self-contained Nature. She is *maya*, the delightful delusion, the dream-like expression of divinity that makes life comprehensible, hence worth living. She is *shakti*, energy, boundless and bountiful.

To realise her is to rejoice in the wonders of life.

Invoke for me, O Agni,
Lakshmi who shines like gold,
is brilliant like the sun,
who is powerfully fragrant,
who wields the rod of suzerainty,
who is the form of supreme rulership,
who is radiant with ornaments
and is the goddess of wealth.

— *Shri Sukta, Rigveda*

Brahma, Vishnu and Shiva who create, sustain and destroy the universe salute Maha-Lakshmi, who embodies the cosmos; Pahari painting.

Lakshmi seated on a lotus
surrounded by white elephants
(symbols of power and fertility)
married couples (symbols of conjugal
bliss and worldliness); Tantrik
painting from Nepal.

Ascent of Lakshmi

Lakshmi is known as the daughter of sage Bhrigu as well as the daughter of Varuna, god of the sea. She is closely associated with Shukra, the guru of *asura*s. At first, she lived with *asura*s, under the ground. Later, she was acquired by *deva*s who reside above the ground. Finally, she became the consort of Vishnu, the preserver of the world. This is how it all came about.

Bhrigu's Daughter

In the beginning, there were three worlds: the celestial regions above, the nether regions below and the earth floating on the sea in between. The *deva*s or gods resided in the celestial regions, the *asura*s or demons in the nether regions and the *manava*s or humans on earth.

To help the inhabitants of the three worlds understand the mysteries of the universe, Brahma revealed the secrets of the Vedas to seven *rishi*s or seers. These *rishi*s were holy beings born out of Brahma's thoughts who could travel between the three worlds. They chanted the *mantra*s of the Vedas during rituals known as *yagna*s and contemplated on the same during austerities known as *tapa*s. Either way, they used the power of the *mantra*s to invoke gods and goddesses and control the workings of the cosmos.

Six of the seven mind-born sons of Brahma used the information given to them by Brahma to invoke Saraswati, the goddess of knowledge, through whose grace mankind acquired enlightenment. However, they soon realised wisdom does not satisfy hunger.

Chapter II

Varuna, the sea-god, who holds a noose in his hand and rides a sea-monster known as *makara*, is described as the father of Lakshmi because all water, hence wealth, comes from the sea; temple carving from North India.

Priests performing *yagna*;
North Indian miniature painting.

Vedic priests invoked two goddesses: the lotus-holding Lakshmi who gave food and the lute-holding Saraswati who gave knowledge. Lakshmi nourished the body, Saraswati nourished the mind. Both were needed to make life worthwhile; modern illustration from a prayer book.

The seventh son, Bhrigu, learnt from Varuna, the god of the sea, that all things are ultimately food and that the world is composed of only those who eat and that what is eaten. He realised the value of food. He used what he had learnt from Brahma to invoke Lakshmi, the goddess of wealth, through whose grace mankind acquired worldly riches.

The Composition of Bhrigu Samhita

The *rishi*s who were learned but poor went to Bhrigu and said, "We know everything about the cosmos, yet the world ignores us. As a result we have no patrons to provide for our material needs."

Bhrigu taught them the art of prediction using astrology or *Jyotisha Shastra*, palmistry or *Rekha Shastra*, geomancy or *Vastu Shastra*, and other occult sciences, collectively known as *Bhrigu Samhita*. He said, "The world needs to see the future to sustain its wealth. In exchange for the information demand all the wealth you need to sustain yourself."

The sages blessed Bhrigu. Since it was his instruction that provided them with a livelihood they concluded that the goddess Lakshmi was his daughter. They addressed her as Bhargavi, she-who-was conceived-by-Bhrigu.

Kavya, the Son of Bhrigu

Bhrigu married Puloma, the daughter of the *asura*-king Hiranakashipu. She was also known as Usha.
They had a son who was called Ushanas, the son of Usha. He was sometimes called Kavya, because he was an extremely gifted poet.

Kavya learnt all that his father had to teach. But he wanted more. So he became the student of *rishi* Angirasa.

Kavya performing *yagna* for the *asura*-king Hiranakashipu; North Indian miniature painting.

Angirasa, however, favoured his son Brihaspati. Piqued, Kavya Ushanas left Angirasa and sought *rishi* Gautama as his teacher.

In time, Brihaspati became lord of the planet Jupiter concerned with logic and rational thought while Ushanas became lord of the planet Venus concerned with intuition and creative thought.

Kavya and Brihaspati Invoke Lakshmi

Indra, king of the *deva*s, appointed Brihaspati as his guru while Hiranakashipu, the king of *asura*s, made his grandson Kavya his guru. Brihaspati lived with the gods in celestial city of Amravati; Kavya lived with the demons in the subterranean Hiranyapura.

Both Kavya and Brihaspati performed *yagna*s to empower their respective patrons. During the ceremony they both chanted the hymn *Shri Shukta* to invoke Lakshmi who ensures victory in battle.

Both *deva*s and *asura*s sought control over Shri, the bounty of earth. Sometimes, the former were successful and sometimes the latter. When the gods won, wealth of the earth was pulled out; when the demons won, wealth of the earth was pulled down. The victor was known as Shriman. Victory was never permanent.

Jupiter or Brihaspati rides an elephant and is the guru of gods. According to Hindu astrology he is associated with logic, rational thought and intellect; modern calendar art.

Kavya and Jayanti

Once Indra sent his daughter Jayanti to seduce Kavya away from the *asura*s. Jayanti's charms had no effect on Kavya. She waited on him nevertheless.

When the *asura*s saw Indra's daughter with their guru, they felt their guru had betrayed them. So they abandoned him. However, without the help of Kavya, they could not obtain the favour of Lakshmi. Without Lakshmi's favour, they lost all battles against the *deva*s.

Realising their mistake, the *asura*s begged Kavya to be their guru once again.

Venus or Shukra, also known as Ushanas and Kavya, rides a horse and is the guru of demons. According to Hindu astrology, Venus is associated with intuition and creativity; modern calendar art.

Lakshmi Charms Narasimha

Determined to be eternally victorious, Hiranakashipu sought immortality. He performed *tapas*, invoked Brahma and obtained a boon by which he could not be killed either by a man or a beast, indoors or outdoors, during the day or at night. Empowered by this boon he defeated the *deva*s in battle.

The *deva*s then invoked Vishnu, the warrior-god, who managed to kill Hiranakashipu taking the form of Narasimha, a being that was neither man nor lion. Narasimha dragged the *asura*-king to the threshold,

Jayanti, the daughter of Indra, trying to seduce Kavya; North Indian miniature painting.

that is neither indoors nor outdoors, and disembowelled him at twilight, that is neither day nor night.

After killing the *asura*-king, Narasimha's rage did not ebb away. He threatened the world with his fury. To calm him down, Brihaspati invoked Lakshmi whose beauty charmed Narasimha into bliss.

Kavya Invokes Shiva

Realising that immortality was not easy to obtain, Kavya decided to learn *Sanjivani vidya*, the science to resurrect the dead, with which he could revive *asura*s slain in battle against the *deva*s.

His guru Gautama advised him to invoke Shiva, the ascetic-god, the only one to possess this secret science. Shiva had used *Sanjivani vidya* to help the moon-god Chandra wax when the latter had been cursed to wane by his father-in-law Daksha for neglecting his wives, the stars.

Kavya decided to invoke Shiva through *tapa*s. He hung himself by the feet over a great fire and contemplated on the ascetic-god.

Lakshmi, the gentle goddess, calmed the fury of Narasimha, the man-lion incarnation of Vishnu; modern calendar art.

14

Kavya Becomes Shukra

After many eons of *tapa*s, Shiva finally appeared before Kavya. When Kavya sought the secret science of resurrecting the dead, Shiva responded by swallowing him.

Trapped in Shiva's body, Kavya sought a route to escape but found to his dismay that the ascetic-god had sealed all the orifices of his body. All except one — the phallic opening. Kavya escaped through it.

When Shiva tried to punish him for escaping, his consort Parvati stopped him. "He has emerged from your body and is now like your son." Shiva accepted Kavya as his son and taught him the secret science of resurrecting the dead.

Since Kavya had emerged from Shiva's manhood, he acquired the name Shukra, the divine seed. Just as seed can produce plants when planted in appropriate soil, Shukra had the power to bring prosperity and power wherever he went.

Kavya performing penances to invoke Shiva and learn the secret of rejuvenation; illustration by author.

Shiva, the ascetic-god, and his consort Parvati. Shiva accepted Kavya as his son, named him Shukra and taught him the secret of reviving the dead; North Indian miniature painting.

15

Vishnu beheading Shukra's mother who had given protection to the demons. For this act of violence against his mother, Shukra cursed Vishnu to be born on earth as a human and experience death; illustration by author.

Kacha, son of Indra (or Brihaspati, according to some texts), approaches Shukra and seeks the secret of rejuvenation; North Indian miniature painting.

Shukra Curses Vishnu

While Shukra was away, the *asura*s had approached his mother Puloma, also known as Kavya-mata, for protection. She decided to cast the spell of sleep on their enemies. When the *deva*s learnt of this they invoked Vishnu who hurled his discus, the Sudarshan *chakra*, and beheaded Kavya-mata before she could utter the magic formula.

When Shukra returned, he found his mother's decapitated remains. All the *asura*s were dead. Using the *Sanjivani vidya*, he revived them all.

For attacking his mother, he cursed Vishnu that he would be born on earth as a mortal in the forms of Parashurama, Rama and Krishna and know the pain of death.

Kacha Tricks Shukra

With Shukra in possession of *Sanjivani vidya*, the *asura*s became very powerful and were able to defeat the *deva*s with ease. To restore the balance of power, it was necessary for the *deva*s to get hold of the secret science. Indra's son Kacha was given the task of doing so.

Disguised as a priest, Kacha enrolled himself as Shukra's student. When Shukra showed no signs of sharing his knowledge, Kacha seduced Shukra's daughter Devayani in the hope of getting access to the secret through her. She knew the formula well though it worked only when chanted by men.

The *asura*s realised what Kacha was up to. So they killed him. Devayani who was by now in love with Kacha begged her father to revive him using the *Sanjivani vidya*. He did so much to his daughter's delight.

Determined to be rid of Kacha, the *asura*s killed him once again and fed him to Shukra. "If I revive him, he will burst out of my body and end up killing me," said Shukra to his distraught daughter. "In that case," said Devayani, "I will teach him the secret of reviving the dead using which he will bring you back to life."

Pleased with his daughter's plan, Shukra revived Kacha and died in the process, as predicted. Devayani taught the secret of *Sanjivani vidya* to Kacha who revived his guru.

Now that he had what he wanted, Kacha decided to leave Shukra's hermitage. Devayani begged him to stay or take her as his wife. "How can I marry you? I was born of your father just as he was born of Shiva. Now I am his son and you are my sister." So saying, Kacha abandoned Devayani and went back to his father's kingdom.

Devayani cursed Kacha that he would never be able to use the knowledge that he had gained through subterfuge. And so, while the *deva*s possessed *Sanjivani vidya*, they could never use it.

Devayani begged her father Shukra to revive her beloved Kacha whom he had eaten unknowingly; illustration by author.

Indra, disguised as a priest, learning from Prahalad, the *asura*-king, the secret of his success; North Indian miniature painting.

Indra Tricks Prahalada

After Hiranakashipu, his son Prahalada became king of the *asura*s. Enlightened by Shukra, Prahalada became so prosperous and powerful that Indra, king of the *deva*s, was forced to abandon Amravati.

Determined to find out what made Prahalada so prosperous and powerful, Indra disguised himself as a priest and sought employment with Prahalada. Prahalada was so pleased with his service that he offered him a boon. "Before I ask for something please tell me the secret of your prosperity and power," requested Indra.

Prahalada said, "I am Shriman, blessed with Shri, hence prosperous and powerful. Shri is Lakshmi, the goddess of wealth and fortune. She resides wherever there is merit. I have acquired merit by performing deeds that are in line with *dharma*, the sacred code of conduct established by Vishnu that ensures order in the cosmos."

After hearing this, Indra asked for Prahalada's merits as his boon.

Prahalada had no choice but to agree. Instantly, his merits departed from him and went to Indra. With his merits, went the goddess Lakshmi. Indra then became Shriman, radiant with power and prosperity. He returned to Amravati triumphant.

Mohini Enchants Virochana

Mohini, the enchantress, a form of Vishnu; temple carving from Belur, Karnataka.

Prahalada's son Virochana obtained from Surya, the sun-god, a crown on which Lakshmi resided permanently. Wearing this crown, Virochana became Shriman.

Led by Virochana, empowered by *Sanjivani vidya* that Shukra possessed, the *asura*s defeated the *deva*s in battle. In despair, Indra sought the help of Vishnu.

Vishnu took a female form known as Mohini, the enchantress, and presented herself to Virochana. The *asura*-king was mesmerised by her ravishing form, her grace, her skill in the art of giving pleasure, and her willingness to satisfy any desire.

Before long, Virochana who was known for his wisdom lost all control over his senses. He began dancing to Mohini's tunes. He even offered her a boon, anything she wished. "Give me your head with the crown that you wear," said Mohini. Virochana, without thinking for a moment, beheaded himself.

Vishnu gave Virochana's crown to Indra who then became Shriman once again.

Indra in the company of *apsaras*. The fondness of the god-king for wine and women often incurred the wrath of sages who cursed him with misfortune; North Indian miniature painting.

Durvasa Curses Indra

One day, the sage Durvasa obtained a garland of eternally fragrant lotuses. He decided to give it to Indra.

When the sage arrived in Amravati, he found Indra totally drunk, amusing himself with his courtesans, too busy indulging himself to bother with a guest. Still, Durvasa offered him the garland. Instead of appreciating it, Indra threw it towards his mount, the white-skinned six-tusked elephant called Airavata.

The elephant picked up the garland with his trunk, threw it on the ground, and trampled it with his feet.

Disgusted by Indra's behaviour, insulted by the way his gift was treated, Durvasa cursed Indra: "You do not respect the wealth and power bestowed upon you. May you be deprived of it all. May Lakshmi abandon you."

Disappearance of Lakshmi

No sooner did Durvasa utter his curse than the goddess of wealth and fortune dissolved herself in the ocean of milk.

Instantly, a pall of gloom descended upon the three worlds: cows stopped giving milk, plants did not bear flower or fruit. The sun did not shine, gems did not sparkle, animals became dull and listless. There was no joy anywhere.

Gods and demons were united in their grief over the disappearance of the delightful goddess.

The gods approached their champion Vishnu who advised them to churn out the goddess from the ocean of milk. "You will need the help of the *asura*s to be successful."

Indra and his elephant-mount Airavata; North Indian miniature painting.

19

Churning of the Ocean

It was an enterprise of cosmic proportions with *deva*s and *asura*s serving as the force and counterforce of the churn. Mount Meru served as the spindle, the serpent Ananta-Sesha was the churning rope and the turtle Akupara was the steady base.

In effect, the gods and demons, the bright and dark forces of the universe, were using the shaft of Space and the beast of Time to churn the essence of existence out of the shapeless substance of life.

Vishnu, the preserver, oversaw the entire project.

The *deva*s and the *asura*s had to churn the ocean for hundreds and thousands of years before they could churn Lakshmi out, for without effort there is no reward. As they churned Brihaspati and Shukra chanted hymns in praise of the goddess.

Lotus-born

Constant friction because of the churning set the trees on Mount Meru alight. The winding and unwinding caused the serpent Ananta-Sesha to vomit out venom. Despite these predicaments, the gods and demons continued without a pause.

Pleased by their determination to strive despite all of the odds, Lakshmi emerged in her full splendour as Shridevi seated on a splendid thousand-petalled lotus.

She looked at once like a nymph and a mother, gentle yet charming. Draped in a red saree, a diamond-studded crown adorned her head. Jewels of every description adorned her body: armlets, bracelets, anklets, nose-rings, finger-rings, toe-rings, necklaces of gold and silver, studded with sapphires, rubies, emeralds and pearls.

All those assembled were stunned by the sheer magnificence of this goddess. Everyone rushed to welcome this beautiful goddess. Gods sang songs. Demons danced in joy. Sages blew conches.

The gods and the demons churning the ocean of milk using the Axis of Space as the spindle and the Serpent of Time as the rope; South Indian temple wall carving.

With the goddess came innumerable gifts — the wonders of life.

The ascent of Lakshmi from the ocean of milk; Tanjore painting.

Gifts of Prosperity

The best of animal, plant and mineral wealth rose in the form of Kamadhenu, Kalpataru and Chintamani. Together they were the perfect symbols of *artha*, worldly wealth.

Kamadhenu was the wish-fulfilling cow whose udders contained every kind of food imaginable.

Kalpataru was the dream-realizing tree whose branches bore every kind of fruit.

Chintamani, the desire-satisfying gem, could turn every dream into reality.

In Lakshmi's arms was a pot called *Akshaya patra* that is always full of grain and gold.

Along with Lakshmi emerged many gifts that represent prosperity, pleasure and power; Tanjore painting.

Gifts of Power

A virile seven-headed flying horse called Ucchaishrava and a strong yet graceful white-skinned six-tusked elephant called Airavata followed Lakshmi.

The sea also released a bow called Sharanga — symbol of poise and discretion, and a conch-shell, the Panchajanya, the trumpet of victory.

These gifts, the goddess reserved for one worthy of cosmic kingship. Using these symbols of worldly power, he had to establish *dharma*, righteous code of conduct across the universe.

Gifts of Pleasure

Lakshmi's son Manmatha, the god of *kama*, pleasurable pursuits, also rose with her. He was handsome with a winsome smile and radiant eyes. He rode a parrot, held a sugarcane bow and five flowery arrows with which he roused the five senses. *Makara*, an aquatic creature that was part fish, part goat and part elephant served as his emblem.

Rambha, a damsel who knew sixty-four ways to pleasure the senses and amuse the mind, accompanied Manmatha. She held a garland of bright and fragrant flowers known as Vaijayanti.

Sura, the goddess of wine, was Lakshmi's handmaiden.

Beside Lakshmi walked Dhanvantari, the divine physician who brought with him the science of health and healing called Ayurveda and also the elixir of immortality, *amrita*. This gift of health allowed the world to enjoy the gifts of Lakshmi.

Dhanvantari, the god of health and healing, emerged from the ocean of milk along with Lakshmi for only with health can wealth be enjoyed; modern calendar art.

Lakshmi Marries Vishnu

The gods, the demons and other celestial beings scrambled to claim the many treasures that had emerged from the sea: the *devas* took the elephant; the *asuras* took the horse; the *rishis* took the cow; the *yakshas*, the tree; the *nagas*, the jewel.

22

Everybody wanted *amrita* and so fought over it. The demons tried stealing it but were tricked into giving it to the gods by the enchantress Mohini, who was none other than Vishnu in disguise. Mohini charmed the *asura*s with her smile. While they were spellbound by her lovely eyes, she distributed the elixir only amongst the gods.

With *amrita* in the hands of *deva*s and *Sanjivani vidya* in the hands of *asura*s, the balance of power in the cosmos was restored.

Nobody claimed the nymph, the wine and the doctor, who as a result became freely available to all.

Only Vishnu sought nothing.

This pleased Lakshmi. She gave him the bow and the conch. Then placing the Vaijayanti garland round his neck, she accepted Vishnu as her eternal consort.

Manmatha, or Kama-deva, the lord of lust and love, who rides a parrot and shoots five flower arrows to arouse the five senses with his sugarcane bow; Ganjifa painting from Maharashtra.

Lakshmi Worships Shiva

Along with the wonderful gifts of the ocean came Halahala, a poison with the power to destroy all living things. Nobody wanted this gift.

Since all other gifts had either been claimed or shared, the gods gave the poison to the hermit-god Shiva who drank and digested it without hesitation.

Lakshmi saluted the god who took what nobody wanted.

Vishnu in the form of Mohini distracting the demons with her beauty while she distributes the nectar of immortality amongst the gods; North Indian miniature painting.

23

Vishnu, the bearer of the conch, discus, mace and lotus with his consort Lakshmi seated in the coils of Ananta-Sesha on the ocean of milk; Pahari miniature.

Detail of image of Venkateshwara, Balaji, of Tirupati, Andhra Pradesh, showing image of Lakshmi and her local manifestation, Padmavati, on his chest. Vishnu is therefore known as 'Shrinivasa' or the abode of Lakshmi.

Lakshmi and Vishnu

Vishnu placed Lakshmi on his chest. Hence he came to be known as Shrinivasa, the abode of Lakshmi. The symbol of Lakshmi on his chest is known as Shrivatsa.

Vishnu held a discus, conch, mace and lotus in his four hands. The discus was a symbol of rhythmic order or *ritu* that he established in Nature; with his conch-shell trumpet, he warned people not to hurt Lakshmi; with his mace he punished all those who hurt Lakshmi; with his lotus he offered the beauty and bounty of Lakshmi.

Vishnu declared that Lakshmi's name must be uttered before his name is taken. She was his *shakti*. Without her he did not have the wherewithal to sustain the world. Without her he was powerless. Hence to invoke Vishnu, devotees say, "Lakshmi-Narayana."

It is through Lakshmi that the devotee approaches Vishnu. Without her, he is unreachable.

Rescue of the Earth-goddess

The earth is the most tangible manifestation of Lakshmi because all wealth ultimately comes from the earth. The earth-goddess **Bhoodevi** is often distinguished from **Shridevi**. Although both are manifestations of Lakshmi, Shridevi bestows wealth that is intangible such as power and kingship, while Bhoodevi bestows wealth that is tangible such as animals, plants and minerals. In South Indian images, the two goddesses are shown on either side of Vishnu or seated demurely at his feet.

Bhoodevi is often visualised as a cow; her milk represents the bounty she offers mankind. This is her story.

Raising of the Earth-goddess

The *asura* Hiranyaksha, brother of Hiranakashipu, laid claim to the earth and her bounty and dragged the earth-goddess under the sea.

Chapter III

Vishnu with his two wives, the two manifestations of Lakshmi, the celestial Shridevi and the earthly Bhoodevi; Chola bronze idols from South India.

Vishnu as the boar-god Varaha raising the earth from the bottom of the sea after killing the demon Hiranyaksha; Pahari painting.

25

The earth-goddess Bhoodevi accepting Varaha as her consort and naming him Bhoo-pati, lord of the earth; temple carving from Gujarat.

Bali, the son of Prahalada and grandson of Hiranakashipu, king of *asuras*; Pahari painting.

Hearing her cries for help Vishnu took the form of a boar, plunged into the sea, gored the demon to death, placed Bhoodevi on his snout and raised her to the surface, to the delight of all earthly creatures.

As the two rose, Bhoodevi accepted Vishnu as her eternal consort and protector. Their embrace caused mountains to form. He plunged his resplendent tusks into the earth and impregnated her with the seed of all plants. He became Bhoopati, lord of the earth.

Bali Conquers the Three Worlds

Bali, son of Virochana, grandson of Prahalada, great grandson of Hiranakashipu, had led the *asuras* who had churned the ocean of milk. He was angry that *deva*s had denied the *asura*s a share of the elixir of immortality.

Determined to restore the glory of the *asura*s, Bali earned great merit through *tapa*s and *yagna* and, in time, became more powerful than any other being in the cosmos.

He overthrew Indra and made himself lord of the three worlds.

Vamana Outwits Bali

Bali's success disturbed the balance of the cosmos. In a balanced world, gods lived in the skies, humans on earth and the demons underneath. In a balanced world, gods and demons experienced success and failure alternately with unfailing regularity. This rise and fall of fortunes established *ritu*, a natural rhythm, enabling the sun to rise and set, the moon to wax and wane, the tide to oscillate, the seasons to change, the plants to wither and bloom.

To restore balance in the three worlds, Vishnu took the form of a dwarf priest and approached Bali for alms. Bali was generous when it came to priests; he offered Vamana anything he wished. "Give me all the land I cover in three paces," said Vamana. Bali agreed.

Instantly, Vamana turned into a giant. With two steps he claimed the skies and the earth. With the third he pushed Bali under the ground back to the subterranean realm where all *asura*s belong.

He was given permission to rise occasionally. Whenever he rose, crops rose with him. In other words, with him rose Lakshmi. So all humans, who had grown to adore him, anticipated Bali arrival. It marked harvest time and was associated with great festivities.

Diwali is the festival associated with the ascent and descent of Bali. People light lamps, burst crackers and distribute sweets to celebrate his arrival along with Lakshmi and his eventual departure.

Shukra Blinded

When kings give land to a priest they express their generosity ritually by pouring water from a pot. When Shukra realised that Bali planned to give land to Vamana, he reduced himself in size, entered Bali's pot and prevented the water from flowing out through the snout, hoping to disrupt the ritual and prevent the transfer of land.

Shukra knew that Vamana was in reality Vishnu seeking to trick Bali with his disguise.

Vamana realised what Shukra was up to. He took a blade of grass, plunged it into the snout of Bali's pot and blinded one eye of the *guru* of the demons. Shukra left the pot howling in agony and Bali ended up giving Vamana the fateful gift.

Since that day Shukra, lord of the planet Venus, is visualised as a priest with only one eye.

Bali offering water to symbolically transfer his rights over three paces of land asked by the divine dwarf, Vamana; North Indian miniature painting.

How Shukra lost one of his eyes; illustration by author.

27

Lakshmi rejoices and accepts
Vamana as her husband after he
takes control of the three worlds
from Bali the demon-king;
Tanjore painting.

Establishment of Civilisation

After the departure of Bali, to ensure regulated use of earth's resources by humans, Vishnu-Bhoopati instructed Manu, the first king on earth, on *dharma*, the rules of civilised society. As per *dharma*, all humans were obliged to perform their duty based on their station in society, *varna*, and stage in life, *ashrama*.

There were four stations in life concerned with spirituality (*brahmana*), politics (*kshatriya*), economics (*vaishya*) and service (*shudra*). There were four stages in life, associated with education (*brahmacharya*), household (*grihastha*), retirement (*vanaprastha*) and asceticism (*sanyasa*).

This *varna-ashrama dharma* ensured proper utilisation of earth's resources, established balance between Nature and culture, maintained stability in society, and enabled all humans to meet the four goals of life: righteous conduct (*dharma*), economic activities (*artha*), pleasurable pursuits (*kama*) and spiritual interests (*moksha*).

Vena Troubles Bhoodevi

King Vena rejected the *varna-ashrama dharma*.
He plundered the earth's wealth without restraint.
Angered by his behaviour, moved by the piteous cries of Bhoodevi, the *rishis* attacked Vena with blades of grass.
By the power of *mantra*, the grass transformed into fiery missiles that killed Vena.

A blinded Shukra weeps as Vamana, the dwarf, becomes Trivikrama, the giant who claims the three worlds with three steps; ivory carving from Kerala.

Establishment of social order by Manu based on *varna-ashrama-dharma*; illustration by author.

29

The *rishi*s then churned out all negative qualities out of Vena's dead body. From what remained they churned out a new, perfect king. He was Prithu, an incarnation of Vishnu. The gods blessed him and gave him a bow, symbol of his sovereignty over earth.

Prithu's Promise to Bhoodevi

Prithu observed that all his subjects were starving as the earth refused to let seeds sprout and plants bear flower or fruit. When he questioned the earth-goddess she accused humans of greed. "Everyone treats me with disrespect and plunders what I offer them."

Prithu begged her for food. She refused. Taking the form of a cow, she ran away.

Prithu followed her with his bow and threatened to shoot her down if she did not comply with his wishes. "If you kill me, your subjects will never get food." Prithu then declared he would use his weapons to punish all those who hurt Bhoodevi. Pleased with this declaration, the earth-goddess let seeds sprout and plants bear flower and fruit. There was food in abundance for all.

Since Prithu had promised to be her protector, Bhoodevi called herself Prithvi. Prithu became the considerate cowherd of the earth-cow, tending to her needs, and milking her with care. He established the practice of

Prithu holding the bow of kingship that gave him divine authority to ensure order on earth; temple carving from South India.

Prithu chasing Bhoodevi who assumes the form of a cow; Pahari painting.

Bhoodevi assumes the form of a cow and begs Vishnu to help her; North Indian miniature painting.

prudent economics and taught mankind how to practice agriculture, animal husbandry and mining without destroying the balance of Nature.

Under Prithu's watchful eye, all creatures milked the earth with consideration. He transformed into the blue sky that watches over the earth.

Burden of Kings

Kings were supposed to uphold *varna-ashrama dharma* in society and punish those who disregarded this sacred code of conduct with force or *danda-nyaya* if necessary. But as time passed duty gave way to desire. Kings became greedy and ambitious, and like Vena, began plundering the earth.

Kamadhenu, the wish-fulfilling cow who rose along with Lakshmi from the ocean of milk; illustration by author.

Taking the form of a cow, Prithvi begged Vishnu to help her. She called out to Vishnu three times. Vishnu therefore decided to descend on earth three times as Parashurama, Rama and Krishna and restored *dharma*.

Vishnu said, "Rather than taking care of you like a considerate cowherd, the kings of earth squeeze your udders thoughtlessly. I promise you that I will help you drink the blood of all those who claim your milk unrighteously."

31

Parashurama, the priest-warrior incarnation of Vishnu who picked up an axe and hacked down unrighteous kings who burdened the earth and troubled Bhoodevi; North Indian miniature painting.

Kamadhenu and Parashurama

The wish-fulfilling cow Kamadhenu who had emerged from the ocean of milk along with Lakshmi was in the care of *rishi* Jamadagni. Towards the end of *Krita Yuga*, the first quarter of the world-cycle, King Kartaviryarjuna, who had been blessed with a thousand arms, decided to claim it by force disregarding the pleas of the sage.

Parashurama, the son of Jamadagni, who was an incarnation of Vishnu, lost his temper when he saw Kartaviryarjuna taking advantage of his military might. He picked up an axe and hacked the thousands-armed king to death.

In retaliation, the king's sons attacked Jamadagni's hermitage and beheaded the sage.

To avenge his father's death, Parashurama declared war against the kings of the world. Only after annihilating five generations of kings and making an offering of blood to his father did Parashurama rest in peace.

Sita and Rama

In the *Treta Yuga*, second quarter of the world-cycle, neither Vali, king of *vanaras*, nor Ravana, king of *rakshasas*, respected *dharma*. They preferred being barbarians

Sita, a domestic manifestation of Lakshmi, sits on the lap of Rama, her husband and protector, who rescued her from Ravana, the patron of jungle laws; modern calendar art.

32

following *matsya nyaya*, the law of the sea and the jungle where might is right and big fish live by eating small fish. Both kings had driven out brothers fearing they were contenders to the throne. Both claimed women by force.

Both were killed by Rama, prince of Ayodhya.

Rama upheld *dharma* at the cost of personal happiness. When his father, in order to fulfill a promise made to his junior queen, ordered him to live in exile in the forest for fourteen years, he obeyed without question.
He abandoned his royal robes, wore clothes of bark and went to the forest followed by his dutiful wife Sita.

Sita was no ordinary woman. She was Bhoodevi's daughter who had been ploughed out of the earth by her father, Janaka, king of Videha.

In the forest, Ravana abducted Sita. To liberate her, Rama befriended the *vanara* Sugriva, who had been driven out of the *vanara*-kingdom Kishkinda by his brother Vali following a misunderstanding. Rama killed Vali, made Sugriva king, established *dharma* in Kishkinda, and with the help of Sugriva's army, launched an attack on Lanka, land of *rakshasas*. After killing Ravana, he crowned Ravana's estranged and righteous brother Vibhishana king of Lanka, established *dharma* in Lanka, and returned triumphant to Ayodhya with Sita by his side.

Rama was crowned king of Ayodhya. During his rule, the Rama-Rajya, *dharma* reigned supreme. Rama became renowned as *maryada purushottama*, the supreme upholder of social values.

Krishna Kills Kamsa

In the *Dwapara Yuga*, the third-quarter of the world-cycle, when the universe was more imperfect than it had been in the earlier two quarters, Kamsa and Jarasandha disregarded *dharma*, preferring to rule by force rather than by consensus. To destroy them, Vishnu took the form of Krishna and descended on earth.

Krishna was born in the family of Yadavas, to Kamsa's sister Devaki, but raised in secret amongst cowherds in Vrindavana to protect him from those who sought to kill him. It was foretold Kamsa would die at the hands of his nephew. At the appointed hour, after surviving many attempts to assassinate him, Krishna entered the city of Mathura, and killed his maternal uncle when the latter challenged him to a wrestling match.

Jarasandha, Kamsa's father-in-law, was so furious that he drove Krishna and his followers out of Mathura. Krishna sought refuge in the island of Dwarka, made friends with the Pandavas, and with their help had Jarasandha killed.

Krishna killing Kamsa who disregarded the law of civilization and ruled by force rather than consensus; Pahari painting.

Krishna with his beloved Radha, who represents the wild and tempestuous manifestation of Lakshmi; temple images from North India.

Krishna, also known as Panduranga, with his chief queen Rakhumai or Rukmini, who represents the domestic and docile manifestation of Lakshmi; temple images from Maharashtra.

Radha and Rukmini

Krishna restored romance in a world that had lost its innocence. He reminded people that the material world was an expression of divine delight. To appreciate its beauty is to appreciate the splendour of divinity.

There were many women in Krishna's life. Two were most prominent: Radha and Rukmini. Both were manifestations of Lakshmi.

Radha, a milkmaid, was Krishna's beloved when he lived amongst cowherds in Vrindavana. Every night, defying social convention, risking infamy, she would slip out of her house and answer the call of Krishna's flute. Together they would dance all night in abandon in the meadow known as Madhuvana on the banks of the river Yamuna.

When it was time to leave his pastoral life behind and move into the world of politics, Krishna bid Radha good-bye and gave his flute up forever.

Rukmini, a princess, was Krishna's wife who sat on his throne when he was in Mathura and Dwarka. She eloped with him to avoid a marriage being forced on her. She bore Krishna many sons including the valiant Pradyumna, who was an incarnation of Manmatha, the god of love.

Both Radha and Rukmini loved Krishna unconditionally. Radha's love was fiery and passionate. Rukmini's was poised and genteel. Radha represented wild and untamed forests; her relationship with Krishna was beyond the restrictions of civilisation, hence secret. Rukmini represented domesticated fields and gardens; her relationship with Krishna was within the norms of society, hence public.

Radha and Rukmini represent the wild and tame aspects of Maha-Lakshmi.

Krishna and Naraka

When Vishnu took the form of the boar Varaha and raised Bhoodevi from the ocean floor, they had produced a son called Naraka.

Naraka was an *asura* who spread havoc in the three worlds. He attacked Amravati, the abode of the *deva*s, and took control of the city. He claimed Indra's parasol as his own and stole the earrings of Aditi, mother of the *deva*s. He even imprisoned 16100 princesses who were in fact village-goddesses.

Krishna riding his eagle with his junior queen Satyabhama by his side to do battle with Naraka, the *asura* son of Bhoodevi; Haveli miniature painting from Rajasthan.

35

Kauravas attempt to disrobe Draupadi after her five husbands, the Pandavas, lost her in a game of dice; miniature painting from Gujarat.

Virapanchali Draupadi who is worshipped in North Tamil Nadu as a manifestation of the earth-goddess in her wild and unbridled state. Her husbands, who represent kings of earth, failed to protect her so she turned to Vishnu, her celestial guardian; temple image from Tamil Nadu.

Indra sought Krishna's help. As he prepared for war, Satyabhama, Krishna's other wife, decided to join him so that she could watch her lord fight.

It was foretold that only Naraka's mother could kill him. In the battle, therefore, Krishna's weapons did not hurt the *asura*. Naraka hurled a lance that hit Satyabhama. Angry, she picked up the lance and hurled it back at Naraka. The *asura* died instantly, for Satyabhama was an incarnation of Bhoodevi.

The death of Naraka liberated all the wealth he had locked in his palace including Indra's parasol, Aditi's earrings and the 16100 princesses who accepted Krishna as their husband.

Draupadi, Bhoodevi Incarnate

The five Pandavas were sons of Kunti, sister of Vasudeva, Krishna's father. The five brothers had a common wife called Draupadi. Neither of them could satisfy her. They sought an explanation from Krishna who said, "Watch her closely in the night when everyone is asleep."

At night, when all were asleep, the Pandavas saw Draupadi leaving the house, entering a forest and transforming into a magnificent but frightening goddess who ate wild buffaloes raw and drank their blood. "Your wife is no ordinary woman," explained Krishna. "She is Bhoodevi incarnate who thirsts for the blood of men who plunder her wealth."

Krishna revealed that each of the five Pandavas had been an Indra in his previous life who ruled the celestial realms and watched over the earth's bounty. They had been reborn to protect Draupadi, the embodiment of worldly riches.

Krishna Rescues Draupadi

Though the five Pandavas were responsible for Draupadi's welfare, they ended up gambling her away.

The victors in the gambling match, the Kauravas, dragged Draupadi by her hair into the gambling hall and in the presence of everyone around proceeded to disrobe her. Her husbands hung their head in shame for they had gambled themselves away too and could not came to her rescue.

Draupadi cried out to Krishna. "When five Indras cannot protect Bhoodevi, she turns to Vishnu, her last refuge and only hope." Instantly, Krishna protected her with a miracle: every garment that the Kauravas removed was replaced by another one, until the Kauravas gave up exhausted. Thus the modesty of the earth-goddess was not violated. Draupadi swore not to tie her hair until she had washed it with the blood of the Kauravas.

The Pandavas lost their rights to their city, Indraprastha, for 13 years. At the end of this period, the Kauravas refused to part with the kingdom. The result was a great war in which Krishna led the Pandavas to victory. During the war, all the Kauravas were killed. Draupadi washed her hair with their blood.

So it came to pass that Bhoodevi drank the blood of kings killed by Parashurama, Rama and Krishna, pleased that Vishnu had fulfilled his promise and destroyed all those who troubled her by disregarding *dharma*.

Krishna protects the earth-goddess Bhoodevi who in the form of a cow nourishes all living things; Patta painting from Orissa.

The earth is a cosmic cow whose milk nourishes all living things, which is why Hindus revere the cow as a form of Lakshmi; modern greeting card illustration.

4	5	6
3		7
2	1	8

Eight forms of Lakshmi that are popular
in South India — (1) Dhana Lakshmi,
(2) Adi Lakshmi (3) Dhanya Lakshmi,
(4) Veera Lakshmi, (5) Gaja Lakshmi
(6) Santan Lakshmi, (7) Vijaya Lakshmi
and (8) Aishwarya Lakshmi; modern
calendar art.

Manifestations of Lakshmi

Chapter IV

Lakshmi provides all that is needed to sustain life. She makes available the best things in the material world. As the absolute glory of Lakshmi cannot be contained in a single form, devotees visualise her in many forms – each form focusing on one aspect of her divinity.

Traditionally, Lakshmi is worshipped in eight forms, each of which offers mankind a much-desired gift or *siddhi*. There is no standard list of these *ashta*-Lakshmis, but it generally includes **Bhagya-Lakshmi**, **Gaja-Lakshmi**, **Dhana-Lakshmi**, **Dhanya-Lakshmi**, **Santan-Lakshmi**, **Vidya-Lakshmi**, **Vira-Lakshmi** and **Vaibhav-Lakshmi**, goddesses of luck, power, wealth, food, children, wisdom, strength and success.

Besides these eight forms, there are many other manifestations of Lakshmi upon which man contemplates.

Adi-Lakshmi: Primeval Mother

Shiva, the destroyer of the world, rose from Brahma's forehead. Brahma, the creator of the world, rises from Vishnu's navel. Vishnu sleeps on the coils of the serpent of time known as Ananta-Sesha. Ananta-Sesha, in turn, floats upon the cosmic waters. And the cosmic-waters? Where do they lie? In what vessel are they contained?

Lakshmi, the affectionate mother of the universe; Mysore painting.

Ancient sages who contemplated on these questions concluded that the container of all life was the womb of the primal mother-goddess, **Adi-Lakshmi**. Also known as **Adi-Shakti**, she existed before everything else. No man, god or demon has the capacity to understand her. She is unfathomable. She is much more than what we know of her.

In the *Brahmanda Purana* it is said that Adi-Lakshmi laid three eggs. From the first egg emerged Ambika and Vishnu. From the second came Lakshmi and Brahma. From the third came Saraswati and Shiva. She gave Saraswati in marriage to Brahma, Lakshmi to Vishnu and Ambika to Shiva. The three couples then went forth creating, sustaining and destroying the universe.

Another text states that from **Adi-Lakshmi** emerged the three qualities or *guna*s of matter: *raja*s or agitation; *tama*s or inertia; and *sattva* or harmony. *Raja*s was embodied in **Maha-Lakshmi**; *tama*s in **Maha-Kali**; and *sattva* in **Maha-Saraswati**.

Adi-Lakshmi, Lakshmi as the supreme mother-goddess; North Indian miniature painting.

Maha-Lakshmi as the *shakti* or power of Vishnu, the god who sustains the cosmos; Mysore painting.

40

Maha-Lakshmi: Consort of Vishnu

Unlike Adi-Lakshmi, Maha-Lakshmi is accessible to the devotee. She is the supreme manifestation of Lakshmi that man, god and demon can perceive, understand and contemplate upon. She represents the benign and bountiful aspect of Nature.

Vishnu, her consort, preserves life using the wealth, wisdom and power she bestows upon him. While he protects the world with his laws, she nurtures it with her love.

Maha-Lakshmi is in many ways similar to the Gnostic goddess **Sophia** or **Shekinah** who personifies the wisdom and splendour of Yahweh or Jehovah, the almighty creator of the world according to Judeo-Christian traditions.

In the Sri-Vaishnava tradition it is said that Maha-Lakshmi is the only way to reach Vishnu and attain *moksha*. In our life we often break *dharma*, the sacred law of Vishnu. The only way to earn his forgiveness is by abandoning ourselves to

Maha-Lakshmi's grace like prodigal children to a mother, for she will plead our case before the divine father. She is visualised seated on the lap of Vishnu as he manifests as the lion (Narasimha), the boar (Varaha) and the horse (Hayagriva).

In *Tantra*, Maha-Lakshmi is less the consort of Vishnu and more an independent entity similar to Durga.

Gaja-Lakshmi: the Goddess of Elephants

In many icons, two white coloured elephants, usually a male and a female, are seen pouring water upon Lakshmi with their upturned trunks. These elephants are one of the eight pairs of *dig-gaja* who stand at the eight corners of the cosmos, holding up the sky. They welcomed Lakshmi when she rose out of the ocean of milk by performing *abhisheka*, ritual consecration. *Abhisheka* is performed to endow an image of a god or the body of a king with divine power. By venerating Lakshmi, the *dig-gaja*s acknowledged her divine capacity to enrich and empower the world. By worshiping her in this form, man does the same.

Elephants are believed to be especially favoured by Lakshmi: they have no natural enemy in the jungle and have greater access to food on account of their size and strength. They have become symbols of strength, grace and royal authority.

In ancient India, only kings could afford to keep elephants. Hence elephants became associated with royalty. Lakshmi, the goddess of sovereignty, is therefore associated with elephants.

Also, in ancient India, elephants were identified with rain-bearing clouds. Indra, lord of thunder, rides *Airavata*, the white-skinned cloud-elephant. Elephants are therefore considered to be companions of Lakshmi, the goddess of fertility.

White elephants, symbols of fertility, pouring water over Lakshmi, the fountainhead of prosperity; modern calendar art.

When Vishnu manifests as the half-lion Narasimha (left), the boar Varaha (center) and the horse-headed Hayagriva (right), Lakshmi always sits with him because he needs her to sustain the cosmos.

Dhana-Lakshmi: Goddess of Wealth

Everyone, except ascetics and mendicants, seeks wealth and property to secure the future.

Vishnu, preserver of life, refused to acknowledge the power of wealth until the day he fell in love with princess **Padmavati** — an incarnation of the goddess Lakshmi. He longed to marry her, but did not have the money to pay for the marriage expenses. Finally he took a loan from Kubera, treasurer of the gods, and vowed not to leave earth until he had repaid the entire amount.

But the interest was so high that the gods feared he would not return to the heavens. They begged Dhana-Lakshmi to liberate the lord. She did, and since that day Vishnu, also known as Daridra-Narayana or the impoverished-lord, is indebted to her.

Padmavati, a parochial manifestation of Lakshmi and the consort of Venkateshwara Balaji, the presiding deity of Tirupati, Andhra Pradesh. To marry her, Balaji who is Vishnu had to take a loan from Kubera, treasurer of the gods, a debt that he continues to repay with the help of offerings made to him; modern calendar art.

Dhanya-Lakshmi: Goddess of Food

Dhanya-Lakshmi is ever present in our kitchens as cereals, pulses, fruits and vegetables. Her presence keeps hunger away.

According to a tale told in South-East Asia, the charming goddess **Shri** rose from the gem on the hood of the cosmic serpent Ananta-Bhoga. But before she could marry her beloved she died. Shedding tears of love, the gods buried her in the forest floor. Out of her head came the coconut palm, from her hands come the banana plant while rice rose from her womb. Hence coconut, banana and rice are considered auspicious fruits or *Shri-phala*.

When Draupadi, queen of Indraprastha, common wife of the five Pandavas, was exiled into the forest with her husbands, Dhanya-Lakshmi gave her a pot that would always be full of food. Thus did the goddess save the impoverished Pandavas from the humiliation of beggary.

Once, Balarama saw Lakshmi visiting the house of a cobbler. "Don't let her enter our house," he told his younger brother Krishna, "She associates with low caste people." Krishna shut the door on Lakshmi's face. "If you keep me out, you will starve," warned Lakshmi. The brothers did not listen. Later, when they entered their kitchen they discovered that all the food there had turned to sawdust. Hungry, they began to beg for food. But every morsel of food offered to them turned to sawdust. Balarama and Krishna realised they had offended Dhanya-Lakshmi and she had walked out of their lives, leaving them hungry. They apologised for not realising the power of the goddess. She forgave them and fed them with her own hands. "I exist in every house. I do not distinguish between rich and poor, priest or cobbler," said Dhanya-Lakshmi.

Krishna and Balarama apologizing to Dhanya-Lakshmi, goddess of food; Patta painting from Orissa.

Raj-Lakshmi: Goddess of Sovereignty

Kingship, the right of one man to rule over others, is believed in many cultures to be a divine gift. The rulers of Babylon worshipped the goddess **Ishtar** whose grace ensured they were victorious in battle and successful in reign. The Bible states that Saul was king of Israel until Yahweh, the supreme divinity of the Judeo-Christian traditions, turned away from him. Zoroastrians believe in Khvaernar, the divine grace that makes kings out of men.

In Hinduism, it is Raj-Lakshmi who confers kingship upon human beings. She grants sovereignty, royal authority and a regal aura to rulers. The kingdom, source of a king's power and splendour, is considered the embodiment of Raj-Lakshmi. Her symbols include: crown, throne, cushions, foot-stool, fly-whisk, fan, umbrella, flag and bow.

Raj-Lakshmi holding the scepter of kingship; Patta painting from Orissa.

Griha-Lakshmi: Goddess of the Household

Every house has a Griha-Lakshmi residing in it.
Her presence fills the house with love and life and
transforms it into a home. Her absence fills the house
with rage, frustration, despair and violence.

A merchant had turned his house into a den of vices.
The merchant's wife **Shrimati** was a pious woman.
One day, at dusk, Shrimati noticed a strange but beautiful
woman dressed in a red sari and holding a pot leaving
the house. On inquiry, the stranger identified herself as
Griha-Lakshmi and said that she was leaving the house as
the man of the house did not value her. Shrimati tried
hard but failed to make Griha-Lakshmi change her mind.
Finally, she said, "Please don't cross the threshold until
I make you an offering of flowers." The goddess agreed
and waited in the house while Shrimati went into the
garden to fetch flowers. In the garden was a well.
The merchant's wife jumped into the well and killed
herself. The goddess of fortune who had promised not to

Griha-Lakshmi, goddess of the
household, resides within the four
walls and transforms the house into
a home; modern greeting card
illustration.

leave until she had received Shrimati's offering of flowers was thus forced to stay in the house for all eternity ensuing its prosperity.

Traditionally, a daughter-in-law is considered a Griha-Lakshmi because on her rests the onus of raising the next generation of the family. In most Hindu marriages when the daughter-in-law enters the house for the first time, conches are blown, lamps are lit and crackers burst to ward off evil spirits. As she steps in, a Marathi bride kicks a pot of rice into the house while an Oriya bride leaves an impression of her foot on the threshold using red-dye, signifying the arrival of good fortune.

Soundarya-Lakshmi: Goddess of Beauty

Rati, Brahma's daughter, was a rather plain looking girl. No man, god or demon found her attractive. Lonely without a lover, she turned to Soundarya-Lakshmi for help. The goddess gave her sixteen love-charms, *the solah shringar*:

1. Bracelets, armlets and bangles of gold to adorn her arms
2. Anklets with bells of silver that jingled as she moved her feet
3. Toe-rings that made her toes look like petals of spring flowers
4. Gem-studded tiaras and hairpins to hold her oiled hair, styled to perfection, in place
5. Necklaces of pearls, diamonds and gold to beautify her neck
6. Earrings to adorn the sides of her head
7. Noserings to enhance the charm of her face
8. Cummerbunds of pearls to enhance the narrowness of her waist
9. Red saree embroidered with gold to drape around her body and accentuate her figure
10. Perfumed pastes to anoint her body and smoothen her skin
11. Bright fragrant flowers for her hair
12. Kohl to darken her eyes
13. Betel nuts and lime wrapped in betel leaf to chew so that her mouth became fragrant and her lips red
14. A black beauty spot on her face, below her lip, to catch the lover's eye
15. Henna and red dyes to paint designs on her palm and soles
16. A red dot, the bindi, symbolising the root of life, reflecting her ability to bear a child, on her forehead

Bedecked with these charms, Rati became the most beautiful woman in the three worlds and won the heart of Manmatha, lord of love. Together they worshipped Soundarya-Lakshmi as the patron of all beautiful things.

Darpan-Sundari, a beautiful nymph holding a mirror; temple wall carving from Hoysala, Karnataka.

A nymph braiding her hair to make herself beautiful; carving from the wall of a step-well in Patan, Gujarat.

45

A couple playing a game of dice which is dependent on the blessings of Bhagya-Lakshmi, goddess of luck; Pahari painting.

Bhagya-Lakshmi: Goddess of Luck

Many believe that six days after a child is born, Bhagya-Lakshmi picks up the newborn and writes his fate upon his forehead. And so in many parts of India, such as Maharashtra where she is known as Satavai, the place where the newborn sleeps is kept clean, decorated with flowers, fruits, milk, lamps and other auspicious items. Some even keep a slate and chalk or a book and pen, to help Bhagya-Lakshmi write the fate of the child.

Bhagya-Lakshmi can also change a man's fortune as Bansi discovered to his delight. Bansi, a street urchin, was walking down the road begging for food when the royal elephant picked him up with his trunk and placed him on his back. To Bansi's surprise, those on the ground who had shooed him away a few moments ago, were now saluting him, for he was the new king! It so happened, the old king had died childless and by ancient law the first man to be raised off the ground by the royal elephant would inherit the crown. In less than a minute Bansi's fortune changed, because Bhagya-Lakshmi had willed it so.

Gambling with dice forms part of rituals venerating Lakshmi because it indicates who is favoured by Bhagya-Lakshmi. The winner at the gambling table is most often a skilled player because fortune favours those most worthy of it.

The seven (sometimes six) virgin nymphs who are worshipped by women seeking children. The eighth image is their son, Skanda; talisman from Maharashtra.

Santan-Lakshmi: Goddess who Grants Children

Children represent the future, heirs of the family fortune. They fill the house with joy. Santan-Lakshmi helps women bear children; she also protects infants from diseases. Some consider her to be **Amba** or **Gauri**, mother of Ganesha.

Known as **Sasthi** in Bengal, she is commonly associated with female cats including tigresses and lionesses because female cats take care of their kittens without the help of their mates, carrying them to hideouts where they are safe from predators. Even in Ancient Egypt, cats were venerated by barren women as the goddess Bastet, bestower of fertility.

Once six maidens became pregnant while bathing in a lake that contained a drop of Shiva's sweat. They gave birth to six lumps of flesh. Not knowing what to do with them, they turned to the goddess Santan-Lakshmi who came to their aid in the form of a cat. She swallowed the lumps of flesh and regurgitated out a virile youth with six heads and twelve arms. He was Sastha, the lord of war. The six maidens, blessed by Santan-Lakshmi, are worshipped as virgin-mothers or *kumari-mata*s by women in many rural communities. They help women become pregnant, prevent miscarriage, aid delivery and protect little children from fatal fevers. Their shrines are found besides lakes and rivers.

A woman holding a child thanks to the grace of Santan-Lakshmi, the goddess who bestows children; carving from the wall of a step-well in Patan, Gujarat.

Vira-Lakshmi: Goddess of Courage

Once Bhairo, a sorcerer, tried to molest a hermitress named Vaishnavi. At first Vaishnavi ran across hills and valleys and hid in caves, hoping that Bhairo would give up the chase. When he did not, she decided to confront him. She picked up a sickle and turned on her pursuer. After a fierce fight, she succeeded in beheading Bhairo. In victory, Vaishnavi transformed into a goddess renowned in the state of Jammu as **Vaishno-devi**. She is often identified as Vira-Lakshmi, the goddess who gives everyone strength to face and overpower the enemy.

Vaishno-devi, who is worshipped in Jammu, is sometimes considered to be a form of Vira-Lakshmi; modern calendar art.

Depicted in icons as bearing weapons and riding a tiger, Vira-Lakshmi is quite similar to Durga, the fierce goddess who killed the buffalo-demon Mahisha. Unlike Durga, however, Vira-Lakshmi is never offered blood sacrifices. Offerings to her are always vegetarian.

While female cats are sacred to Santan-Lakshmi, the male cat or tom-cat is domesticated by Vira-Lakshmi. She confronts his ferocity, domesticates and rides him. Hence, the mount of Vira-Lakshmi is either a lion or tiger.

Go-Lakshmi, the cow form of the goddess who nourishes all living creatures; modern calendar art.

Go-Lakshmi: Cow-goddess

Cows give milk from which one can make curd, butter and ghee. In ancient pastoral societies, cows held great economic significance, and were worshipped as Go-Lakshmi. Cows are called **Kamadhenu**, wish-fulfiller, because a person who possess a milch cow does not depend on anyone for his basic needs of life.

Once, to test the power of Lakshmi, the gods asked her to go and live in the dung of cows. She did so and instantly cow-dung became a valuable source of fuel and manure and an important ingredient in the making of plaster. Since that day, in many festivals, women mould images of Lakshmi out of cow dung and worship her. Before sowing, seeds mixed with milk and dung are worshipped by farmers' wives.

Vidya-Lakshmi: Goddess of Learning and the Arts

Vidya-Lakshmi is that manifestation of Lakshmi who helps transform knowledge into wealth. Like Saraswati, she is viewed as the goddess of learning and the arts. However, while Saraswati patronizes pure knowledge aimed at spiritual growth, Vidya-Lakshmi patronizes knowledge for material advancement.

Krishna and Rukmini worshipping the cow-goddess; modern calendar art.

Thus there is a difference between the two goddesses. By the grace of Saraswati, knowledge and the arts help us appreciate the meaning of existence and discover the divine. By the grace of Vidya-Lakshmi, the scholar uses his learning and the artist uses his art to earn a livelihood.

48

Saraswati's knowledge is transcendental; Vidya-Lakshmi's knowledge is functional.

There is a close relationship between wealth and knowledge. Knowledge helps in creation, acquisition and redistribution of wealth. Wealth supports arts and educational institutions. Wealth sustains life. Knowledge as well as the arts gives meaning to life. Thus, wealth and knowledge need each other in the quest for a spiritually satisfying and materially fulfilling life.

Vasudha-Lakshmi: Earth Goddess

Vasudha-Lakshmi or Bhoodevi is also called **Dharini**, the foundation, for she bears on her back the burden of life. She is supposed to be very patient, strong and submissive. But when men take advantage of her riches and become greedy or arrogant, she refuses to bear their weight. She takes the form of a cow and begs Vishnu, her guardian, to protect her. He does so taking the form Parashurama, Rama and Krishna. Sometimes, Bhoodevi takes the matter into her own hands, letting her fury show through earthquakes and volcanoes.

At one time this earth-goddess was known as Ekanamsa who had two consorts: the dark herdsman Vasudeva and the fair farmer Baladeva — gods of the two basic economic activities known to man: animal husbandry and agriculture. Both these gods are incarnations of Vishnu and the represent the way man relates to the earth throughout the animal and plant kingdoms.

Saraswati and Vidya-Lakshmi are often confused; the former is goddess of pure knowledge while the latter is goddess of commercial knowledge; modern calendar art.

Vasudha-Lakshmi or Bhoo-Lakshmi who is the earth takes the form of Ekanamsa and is flanked by the herdsman Krishna and the farmer Balarama who represent the primary economic activities of mankind, namely animal husbandry and agriculture; 9th century stone carving from North India.

Deepa-Lakshmi, the goddess of lamps who brings light where there is darkness; modern greeting card illustration.

Deepa-Lakshmi: Lamp Goddess

In the dark, man sits still, unable to see his path or do anything. In the dark, plants cannot grow and hence animals cannot survive. Darkness is considered to be inauspicious; it symbolises ignorance and inertia. Light on the other hand signifies vitality, order and life. Lakshmi resides in every lamp and brings light and warmth into everyone's life. Lamps are lit on every auspicious occasion: birth, marriage, festivities, where the presence of Lakshmi is sought. However when there is a calamity, like death, lamps are blown out.

Arogya-Lakshmi: Goddess of Health

When Lakshmi was churned out of the ocean of milk, she rose with Dhanavantari, the god of health and healing, who is a manifestation of Vishnu. Dhanavantari brought to the world *Ayurveda*, the science of longevity and *amrita*, the nectar of eternal life. Arogya-Lakshmi represents that aspect of Lakshmi which bestows good health on a family. Without health the pleasures of life have no meaning.

Kadak-Lakshmi: Fierce Goddess

Kadak-Lakshmi is a rather fierce manifestation of the goddess that is popular in rural India. Lakshmi transforms herself into Kadak-Lakshmi every time a woman is abused by society; she casts the spell of drought or disease on the guilty community. Villagers offer her gifts, feed her sour lemons and pungent chillies, and undergo ritual self-mortification such as walking on fire and rolling on the ground so that she sheds her malevolent or 'hot' form known as **Jari-Mari** and becomes the 'cool' **Shitala**, her benevolent self. The word *kadak* means tough indicating how difficult it is to please Lakshmi.

Kadak-Lakshmi is a rural and wild manifestation of Lakshmi, sometimes associated with Alakshmi, who is appeased with blood sacrifices and offerings of sour and pungent food like lemons and chilies; wooden image from Andhra Pradesh.

50

Lakshmi's Sister

The Atharva Veda refers to two Lakshmis: **Papi-Lakshmi** and **Punya-Lakshmi**. It also provides spells and incantations to drive away the former:

> "Go away, go away Papi-Lakshmi,
> Go and attach yourself to my enemies.
> O Savitar,
> Use your golden hands
> And pluck away this unenjoyable goddess,
> Who clings like a parasite to a tree"

Known as **Alakshmi** in the *Purana*s, Papi-Lakshmi is the inauspicious counterpart of the auspicious goddess Punya-Lakshmi.

Lakshmi's Older Sister

Alakshmi brings poverty and misery in her wake. Nobody likes her.

Some texts describe her as being cow-repelling, antelope-footed, bull-toothed. Others say she has dry shriveled up body, sunken cheeks, thick lips and beady eyes and that she rides a donkey.

Though she is ugly, though she is the goddess of misfortune, nobody dares revile or abuse Alakshmi, for she is Jyestha, Lakshmi's older sister. Instead people offer her prayers and respectfully request her to stay out of their lives.

Chapter V

Lakshmi with her sister Alakshmi; stone carving from North India.

Alakshmi or Papi-Lakshmi or Kadak-Lakshmi, the malevolent and fierce form of Maha-Lakshmi who is feared and has to be appeased lest she brings misfortune; temple wall carving from Orissa.

The sullen Alakshmi who must never be allowed to enter the house as she brings with her strife, sloth and misfortune. To keep her out sour lemons and pungent chillies, generally considered inauspicious, are hung outside the door so that her hunger is satisfied and she loses the urge to enter the house; illustration by author.

Dantura, a malevolent form of the mother-goddess who is invoked through Tantrik rites, is believed to be none other than Alakshmi; 10th century stone carving from Orissa.

The two sisters, though total opposites, love each other. In many scriptures it is clearly mentioned that without propitiating Alakshmi, one cannot please Lakshmi. In rituals the two are worshipped together; the goddess of fortune is invited in while the goddess of misfortune is requested to stay out.

Birth of Alakshmi

According to the *Brahmana* texts, both goddesses rose out of the austerities of Prajapati: Lakshmi rose from his radiant face, while Alakshmi rose from his gloomy back.

In the *Purana*s that describe the emergence of Lakshmi from the ocean of milk, Alakshmi is said to have risen from the venon *Kalakuta* that the serpent Vasuki spat out.

Keeping out Alakshmi

Once the two goddesses visited a merchant and asked him, "Who do you think is more beautiful — Lakshmi or Alakshmi?"

The merchant was in a fix; he knew the penalty for angering either goddess. So he said, "I think Lakshmi is beautiful when she enters my house and Alakshmi is beautiful when she leaves my house."

On hearing this Lakshmi rushed into the merchant's house, while Alakshmi ran out. As a result the merchant's business boomed, profits soared, money poured in and with it came power, prestige and position.

Alakshmi likes to eat sour and pungent things. Merchants in many parts of India tie lemons and green chillies on the doorways of their shops in the hope that when the goddess of misfortune comes to their doorstep, she will eat her favourite food and turn around satiated, without casting her malevolent eye into the shop.

Sour food is avoided during festivals because it is associated with misfortune. Sweet food is offered to sweeten the tongue and invoke the goddess of luck and fortune.

Kadak-Lakshmi and Soumya-Lakshmi

It is believed that the stern Kadak-Lakshmi and the compassionate Soumya-Lakshmi are in fact Alakshmi and Lakshmi, the dark and radiant aspects of Maha-Lakshmi.

In villages, through rituals of self-mortification, blood sacrifice and offerings of bridal finery, bitter neem leaves, sour and pungent food like lemons and chillies, Kadak-Lakshmi is appeased and Soumya-Lakshmi is beckoned. In places where blood sacrifices are no longer performed, pumpkins are smeared with tumeric and red *kumkum* powder and cut to please Kadak-Lakshmi.

In the month of *Kartika* (following Diwali), villagers in many parts of India, sacrifice male buffaloes and bulls, mix the blood and meat with rice and cast the mixture along the frontier of the village in the hope that the offering will please Alakshmi who will stay outside the village and not strike the village with death, disease or drought.

Alakshmi's Home

Once when Alakshmi found Lakshmi living happily with Vishnu in the paradise called Vaikuntha, she cried, "Though I am elder to Lakshmi, I have neither husband nor home."

Feeling sorry for her sister, Lakshmi decreed, *"Mrityu*, god of death, decay and degeneration will be Alakshmi's husband and she will dwell wherever there is dirt, ugliness, sloth, gluttony, envy, rage, hypocrisy, greed and lust."

And hence those who want Alakshmi to stay out of their lives must clean their house and their hearts.

It is said Alakshmi does not like cleanliness, light, heat, fragrance, sound and sweetness. So, at dawn and dusk each day, Hindu women clean the house, light lamps and incense sticks, ring bells, blow conches and offer sweets to all.

Two More Sisters

In ancient Babylon, that stood between the rivers Tigris and Euphrates in the Middle East (modern Iraq), there were two divine sisters not unlike Lakshmi and Alakshmi. They were called **Ishtar** and **Ereshkigal**, the goddess of life and the goddess of death.

Both sisters loved a man called Tammuz and fought over him. Ishtar wanted him to be alive and by her side. Ereshkigal wanted to kill him so that he could live in the kingdom of the dead forever.

After a heated battle, they came to an agreement. For half the year, Tammuz lived with one sister and then spent the rest of the year with the other.

When Ishtar courted Tammuz, it was spring; when they were locked in embrace, it was summer. When Tammuz died, the goddess of life shed tears with the autumn leaves and in winter, when the land was barren and dry,

Devotees are warned to be wary of Lakshmi's owl, which is believed to represent Alakshmi and symbolize arrogance and stupidity that often accompanies fortune and heralds misfortune; modern calendar art.

The two forms of the goddess that represent the waxing and waning aspects of the cosmos bringing fortune and misfortune respectively: the former is sought, the latter shunned; illustration by author.

53

Ishtar, the goddess of food and fortune in Ancient Mesopotamia, brought summer harvest when she was with her beloved Tammuz and winter sterility when she mourned his departure to the kingdom of Ereshkigal, her twin sister who was goddess of death and misfortune.

the Babylonians believed Tammuz was with the goddess of death.

Ancient Greeks also were familiar with this myth that explained the cycle of seasons. They knew Ishtar as Aphrodite, Ereshkigal as Persephone and Tammuz as the handsome Adonis.

Hindu scriptures do not refer to a similar myth but some say that Holi, the festival of spring, marks the return of Manmatha, god of love and pleasure, who is Lakshmi's son, after his annual demise in winter. Bonfires are lit on the eve of Holi to remember how he was killed by a glance of the ascetic Shiva's fiery third eye. The next day, water and red colour is thrown around in revelry to commemorate the revival of Manmatha as the hermit Shiva marries Parvati and becomes a householder. Thus Kama-*deva*'s death is associated with asceticism and his life with worldliness.

The concept of twin sisters who represent the fertile and barren aspects of Nature is reflected in Hinduism in the forms of Lakshmi and Alakshmi.

The death of Kama-deva represents sterility and winter in Hinduism while his rebirth, which is celebrated during Holi, represents the return of fertility and spring; illustration by author.

54

Companions of Lakshmi

In art, Lakshmi stands either independently or in the company of gods such as: Ganapati, the elephant-headed god who removes obstacles, Saraswati, goddess of learning and the arts; Vishnu, her eternal consort, and his many manifestations. Lakshmi is also associated with *naga*s, *apsara*s, *yaksha*s and *asura*s.

Vishnu

Vishnu, the sustainer of the cosmos, is Lakshmi's consort. In art she is shown either residing on his chest, seated beside him, on his lap or at his feet.

Vishnu protects the world; Lakshmi nurtures it. He is the righteous father; she is the compassionate mother. He is the blue sky watching over Lakshmi, the red earth.

Vishnu holds in his hands weapons such as the Kaumodaki mace, the Sudarshana discus, the Sharanga bow, the Nandaka sword, symbols of *danda-nyaya* or force of law by which he establishes *dharma* in the cosmos. This *dharma* gives a sense of predictability and rhythm known as *ritu* in the cosmos making life tolerable despite constant change. When *dharma* is upheld he reclines on the coils of the Ananta-Sesha, the cosmic serpent; when it is disregarded he rides his eagle Garuda to do battle with the forces of anarchy.

Lakshmi sits domesticated at the feet of Vishnu (left) or on his lap (right); North Indian miniature paintings.

Lakshmi in her celestial and earthly forms – Shridevi and Bhoodevi – at the feet of Vishnu; Tanjore painting.

Saraswati, goddess of learning; modern calendar art.

When Vishnu sleeps, the whole world dissolves. When he awakens, the world evolves. When Vishnu sleeps, Lakshmi is Yoganidra, the cause of sleep. When Vishnu awakens, Lakshmi is Yogamaya, the power of creation.

It is said Lakshmi massages Vishnu's feet to envigorate his limbs tired fighting the forces of *adharma*. By placing Lakshmi at his feet, Vishnu prevents worldly riches and power getting to his head. In other words, he keeps Lakshmi in check knowing fully well the power of wealth to corrupt.

When Vishnu takes the form of the lion-headed Narasimha or the boar-headed Varaha to kill demons, when he becomes the horse-headed Hayagriva to enlighten the gods and sages, Lakshmi sits on his lap to calm and inspire him.

Saraswati

Wealth has no meaning without the knowledge to use it wisely. Since wealth and wisdom are equally important to manage worldly affairs, in many images Vishnu, the cosmic-king, is shown flanked by the goddess of wealth Lakshmi as well as the goddess of wisdom Saraswati.

In households and business establishments, the image of Lakshmi is always kept with the image of Saraswati. This practice ritually expresses an intention of the devotee: he wants worldly riches from Lakshmi but he needs the tact to use it from Saraswati.

It is said that Saraswati resides on Vishnu's tongue while Lakshmi sits at his feet.

Saraswati's symbols contrast those of Lakshmi's. She wears white sari; Lakshmi wears red. She does not care about adornments; Lakshmi bedecks herself with jewels and cosmetics. She holds in her hand books, pens, memory beads and musical instruments like the lute; Lakshmi holds the lotus flower and pots. She rides a swan; Lakshmi remains seated on a lotus. Saraswati is associated with the wind (unbound and free); Lakshmi is associated with earth and water (bound and flowing).

Lakshmi is associated not only with her consort, Vishnu, but with many other male divinities including Ganesha, Indra and Kubera. In contrast, Saraswati is associated only with Brahma, a god who is not worshipped, and is very rarely shown in images sitting beside him. When they are seen together, the relationship seems less conjugal and more intellectual.

Lakshmi and Saraswati constantly argue with each other. Lakshmi is concerned with material pursuits; Saraswati with intellectual ones. Lakshmi resides with traders and in market places; Saraswati resides with teachers and in schools.

Rare image from one of the few Saraswati temples in India at Basara, North Andhra Pradesh.

Saraswati, the goddess of knowledge, with Brahma, the creator. With her help, he creates the world. Through his four heads she emerges as the four Vedas; 19th century illustration.

57

*Naga*s or serpent-gods once rolled on drops of *amrita*, nectar of immortality, and hence can replace old skin with new skin to rejuvenate themselves. They are therefore symbols of earth's renewable fertility; village shrine under a Banyan tree in South India.

*Naga*s

*Naga*s are hooded serpents. Because they slither on the ground and slip into cracks and crevices, they are believed to have an uncanny relationship with earth's fertility. Just as soil recovers its fertility year after year, so do serpents rejuvenate themselves month after month by shedding their skin.

For thousands of years, in cultures all around the world, serpents have been associated with the energies and powers governing the mysteries of life and death. Even today a serpent is the internationally recognised symbol of medicine.

*Naga*s are considered to be guardians of Lakshmi's grace. They are petitioned by barren women seeking children and farmers seeking a rich harvest.

Termite-hills are said to be the entrances to the subterranean land of serpents known as *Naga-loka* or Bhogavati. Hence termite-hills are greatly revered by Hindus. In Bhogavati is *naga-mandala*, a palace of gems, abode of Vasuki, king of serpents. Vasuki's sister Manasa is often petitioned to protect people from snake bites.

Because Ananta-Sesha, the divine serpent, served as a churning rope and suffered greatly to help draw Lakshmi out of the ocean of milk, every serpent was rewarded with a gem. According to folk belief, these *naga-mani*s located on the hood of serpents have the ability to cure any disease and fulfil every wish because in these gems resides the spirit of Lakshmi.

Termite hills are believed to lead one to the abode of *naga*s, serpent-gods who are keepers of fortune-bestowing gems; modern calendar art.

*Asura*s

In narratives, it is constantly stressed that the *deva*s or gods obtained Lakshmi from the *asura*s or demons. The *asura*s of Hinduism are not evil creatures like the demons of the biblical tradition. They are children of

Brahma who live under the earth and who pull the earth's wealth downward. The gods who live above the earth pull wealth upwards.

*Asura*s live in Hiranyapura, the city of gold, indicating their close association with mineral wealth. They possess *Sanjivani vidya*, the secret of regeneration, indicating their association with plant wealth.

Agni, the fire-god, fights the *asura*s, melts rocks and releases minerals in favour of humans. Indra, the thunder-god, causes rain to fall so that crops rise out of the soil.

Since the action of *deva*s favours mankind they are referred to as 'gods', while their enemies are regarded as 'demons'.

In epics, Vishnu and his incarnations, Shiva and his sons, and Durga in her many forms fight with *deva*s against *asura*s, not because the demons are bad or morally inferior, but because the victory of the gods releases wealth hoarded by demons and hence supports life on earth. Prayers are offered to the sun-god Surya, moon-god Chandra, wind-god Vayu, rain-god Indra, fire-god Agni and other *deva*s for the same reason.

Before judging *asura*s, it must be kept in mind that *asura*-kings like Prahalada, Virochana and Bali are renowned for their devotion, wisdom and generosity, while the king of *deva*s, Indra, and the other gods are infamous for their love of wine and women.

In Bhagavata Purana, Vishnu says that to release Lakshmi from the ocean of milk, the gods needed the help of the demons. This is because while gods could release and distribute wealth, only the demons knew how to regenerate wealth. In the language of modern economics, one might say that *deva*s are distributors of wealth while *asura*s are creators of wealth. The former spend wealth, the latter hoard it. Both play vital roles in the cycle of wealth.

An *asura* holding a *naga*; modern sculpture in Karnataka.

*Asura*s represent subterranean forces that possess *Sanjivani vidya* with which they can resurrect the dead and regenerate wealth. Since they hoard this wealth, they are considered demons; North Indian painting.

59

*Gandharva*s, celestial musicians; 10th Century temple wall carving from Rajasthan.

*Apsara*s and *Gandharva*s

*Apsara*s are divine damsels, courtesans who entertain the gods. They are patrons of the sixty-four arts — including music, dance, painting, sculpture, cuisine, erotics, fashion, perfumery — which rouse the senses, titillate the flesh and amuse the mind. They personify the pleasures of life and the luxuries that come with wealth.

*Apsara*s rose from the ocean of milk with Lakshmi. Like wealth, they belong to nobody. Their association with affluence, power, luxury, beauty and allure, made them auspicious. Their earthly counterparts, the *deva-dasi*s and *ganika*s of yore, were therefore venerated in ancient times and invited to participate in certain sacred ceremonies like marriage and childbirth. Mud from their houses were used to mould idols of the goddess. It was also sprinkled on the foundation of new buildings to usher in good fortune.

Apsa means water in Sanskrit. *Apsara*s, like Lakshmi, are associated with water bodies such as ponds and rivers. These nymphs are mercurial creatures; like water they slip out of the hand. Apsaras represent the delightful but transient nature of all material things. Their companions are the *gandharva*s, the fragrant ones, who are celestial

*Apsara*s flying in the woods; North Indian miniature painting.

musicians and associated with flowers and nectar. When *gandharva*s make music, the *apsara*s dance. *Apsara*s and *gandharva*s are companions of Manmatha, the lord of love and pleasure, who is Lakshmi's son.

Manmatha

Manmatha is the god of love, lust, sensual pursuits and fertility. He is described as the son of Vishnu and Lakshmi in the Harivamsa. He is described as a beautiful god who rides a parrot and carries a banner with the symbol of *makara*, a mythical beast that is part fish, goat and elephant. He has a sugarcane bow. The bowstring is made of bees. He has five flowers for arrows with which he arouses the five senses.

Rati and Priti, goddesses of the erotic art and romantic love, are his consorts. Vasanta, the god of spring, is his best friend.

Manmatha shot an arrow into the ascetic Shiva's heart. Enraged, Shiva burnt him to death with a glance of his fiery third eye. Manmatha, however, was reborn as soon as Shiva embraced Shakti, the mother-goddess, and abandoned his ascetic ways to become a householder.

Invoke for me O Agni,
that goddess Lakshmi,
who is ever unfailing,
being blessed by whom I shall win:
wealth in plenty,
cattle, servants, horses,
and men.

— *Shri Sukta, Rigveda*

Manmatha or Kama-deva, the son of Lakshmi, holding symbols of fertility such as the parrot, sugarcane bow, flower-tipped arrows and a flag displaying his emblem, the elephant-headed fish known as *makara*; illustration by author.

Yakshas and Rakshasas

*Yaksha*s are keepers of mineral wealth and gems. They live within trees and in lakes and guard secret treasures. They are very fond of riddles; those who solve their puzzles are richly rewarded but the rest are stricken with madness. A *yakshi* or *yakshini*, a female *yaksha*, is greatly feared by men because she lures them with the temptation of gold, only to kill them when they try to embrace her.

*Yaksha*s are often described as 'water' gods because of their corpulent form. On temple walls they are depicted as rather obese and sometimes deformed, indicating that their body is full of water. Water is necessary for plants to grow. Where there is water there is life. This makes *yaksha*s the guardians of life-giving principles.

Massaging the pot-belly of a *yaksha* is said to bring good fortune.

*Yaksha*s are closely related to the *rakshasa*s. Brahma's son Vaishrava had two wives. One of them gave birth to the race of *yaksha*s while the other gave birth to the *rakshasa*s.

Ravana, the king of *rakshasa*s, who used force to seize control of the city of gold, Lanka, from his half-brother Kubera, king of *yaksha*s; Tanjore painting.

Images of male and female *yaksha*s who live in trees; ancient North Indian stone pillars.

62

*Yaksha*s or pot-bellied misshapen forest spirits who guard treasures and secret wealth; temple carving from South India.

Both were forest beings associated with the wealth of the forest. Both live in cities of gold. Man tames the wilderness, turns forest into fields, in his quest for wealth; this often brings man in conflict with *yaksha*s and *rakshasa*s.

Kubera

In many texts, Lakshmi is closely identified with Kubera. He is sometimes her companion, her servant, her brother or even her consort.

Kubera is the king of *yaksha*s who lives in Alakapuri, a radiant city located somewhere amidst the northern hills. He is the guardian of the northern direction. He is also treasurer of the gods.

Like all *yaksha*s, Kubera is extremely fat. He sports a plump chin and has a protruding-belly. His obesity is a sign of his affluence for only he can afford to spend all his time eating and sleeping instead of trying to earn a living.

Kubera always carries a bag filled with gold and nine priceless gems — the *nav-ratna* — pearl, diamond, ruby, sapphire, emerald, coral, topaz, crystal and garnet. Kubera is also the lord of nine treasures — *nav-nidhana*.

According to the *Ramayana*, the golden city of Lanka was built by Kubera. He was driven away by Ravana, king of the *rakshasa*s, who then became lord of Lanka. Ravana travelled across the world in *pushpak-vimana*, a flying chariot studded with jewels of every kind that was built by Kubera.

Kubera's pet mongoose spits out jewels whenever it opens its mouth. Riddhi and Nidhi, goddesses of material growth and accumulation, are his consorts. The image of Kubera and his consort can be seen gracing the headquarters of the Reserve Bank of India at New Delhi.

While Vishnu rides an eagle and Shiva a bull, Kubera rides a man — the slave of wealth.

Indra once came to Kubera because he needed money. He found Kubera collecting grains of rice from the kitchen floor. "A man who collects grains of rice from the kitchen floor cannot be rich enough," said Indra. Kubera

Kubera, king of the *yaksha*s, who is treasurer of the gods and holds a bag of gold in his hand; stone idol from North India.

63

Kubera, the plump treasurer of the
gods, with his consort Nidhi, goddess
of treasures, blessed by Lakshmi.
He is surrounded by the nine planets
of Fate, piles of grain, gold, gems and
water, symbols such as conch, lotus
and fish. He holds the golden
mongoose, which keeps spitting gems
and has the symbol of Venus, the
horse, on his throne; modern calendar

art from South India.

replied, "I am the richest god only because I collect every grain of rice that others overlook." Indra thus realised the power of thrift.

Once Kubera became so proud of his wealth that he claimed he could buy anything in the world. To teach him a lesson Shiva plucked out one of his eyes. Kubera soon realised that money cannot buy everything, certainly not an eye. He replaced his lost eye with a false one made of gold to remind himself about the importance of humility. He is therefore called Pingalaksha, golden-eyed.

At another time, Kubera told Shiva, "Why do you live in poverty like a hermit? I can give you all the wealth you need." To teach him a lesson, Shiva requested him to feed his son Ganapati. Ganapati ate everything in Kubera's house and still asked for more food. Exasperated, Kubera ran to Shiva who told him that pride is the prime cause for loss of wealth and dignity.

River-Goddesses

River goddesses such as the *makara*-riding Ganga and turtle-riding Yamuna are often described as the daughters of Lakshmi as they bring life and wealth on their banks.

Ganga, the river-goddess who rides the elephant-headed dolphin-like *makara*, represents the life-giving as well as ever-flowing, mercurial and ephemeral nature of material things; Kalighat painting.

Shiva, the cosmic ascetic, meditates on an elephant skin, indicating his disdain for the principle of fertility. The river-goddess Ganga is bound in his hair indicating how his detachment helps him control the mercurial nature of material things; Pahari painting.

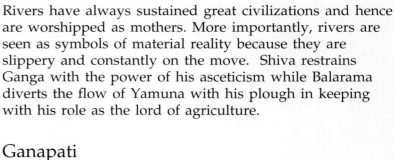

Ganesha, as god of success, with his two consorts Buddhi or Siddhi and Riddhi (personifications of intellectual, spiritual and material success) who hold his sons Shubha and Labha (personifications of luck and profit); Kalamkari cloth painting.

Rivers have always sustained great civilizations and hence are worshipped as mothers. More importantly, rivers are seen as symbols of material reality because they are slippery and constantly on the move. Shiva restrains Ganga with the power of his asceticism while Balarama diverts the flow of Yamuna with his plough in keeping with his role as the lord of agriculture.

Ganapati

Ganapati, the elephant-headed god who presides over thresholds and wards off obstacles, is often found sitting beside Lakshmi.

Like a *yaksha*, Ganapati has a stocky built, short plump limbs and a protruding belly. But he has something that other *yaksha*s do not — wisdom, using which he heralds prosperity. This makes him Lakshmi's favourite companion.

Ganapati has so much intelligence that he requires the head of an elephant to contain it. With his large ears, he hears everything and keeps accumulating more knowledge. His trunk is turned to the left, out of the way of his right hand with which he writes down books of sacred wisdom.

Lakshmi is often worshipped along with Ganapati when businessmen open new account books as Lakshmi brings auspiciousness and luck (*shubha*) and profit (*labha*) when Ganapati removes all obstacles; modern calendar art.

66

Lakshmi flanked by Saraswati and Ganesha indicating prosperity arrives when there is knowledge and no obstacles. That the goddess of wealth wears a green, rather than red, sari associates her with Ganesha's mother Gauri, the maternal aspect of the mother-goddess; modern calendar art.

Santoshi, the goddess of satisfaction, who is the daughter of Ganapati, is worshipped on Fridays with offerings of jaggery and a taboo on sour food; modern calendar art.

Lakshmi with her two pot-bellied affluent companions, Ganapati (left) and Kubera (right); stone carving from North India.

Long ago, farmers were very unhappy because mice were burrowing into their granaries and stealing their corn. Ganapati gave them serpents who ate the mice and stopped the plunder. Ganapati thus got rid of the problem that was blocking the prosperity of man.

Ganapati's role as the remover of hurdles and the envoy of fortune is expressed iconographically by showing a mouse (symbol of problems) cowering at its feet and a serpent (symbols of earth's fertility) winding around his pot-belly (symbol of affluence).

Ganapati's elephant head symbolises unstoppablity: no one can stop an elephant from getting anywhere.

Symbols of fertility, hence Lakshmi, are an integral component of Ganapati worship. These include pots filled with water, rice, banana plant, coconut, mango leaves, *dhurva* grass, jaggery, swastika and marigold flowers.

Ganapati is said to have two consorts called Siddhi (spiritual prowess), also known as Buddhi (spiritual insight) and Riddhi (material abundance). His sons are called Shubha (auspiciousness) and Labha (profit). His daughter is Santoshi (satisfaction). His association with Lakshmi is thus natural.

Some scholars believe that over time Ganesha's consorts Riddhi and Buddhi transformed into Lakshmi and Saraswati.

Attributes of Lakshmi

In art, Lakshmi is characteristically visualised as a beautiful lady with four hands, dressed in red saree, decorated with gold ornaments, holding a pot, seated on a lotus flower, flanked by white elephants who shower water over her with their trunk. She is often shown in the company of Ganesha, remover of obstacles, and Saraswati, goddess of knowledge and the arts.

The symbols of Lakshmi define her cosmic role. They help us understand her better.

Physical Form

Lakshmi has the colour of turmeric and gold, so she is described as glowing with prosperity.

Lakshmi has four hands in which she holds lotuses and pots of grain and gold. With one upward-pointing hand she blesses her devotees. With her other downward-pointing hand she showers devotees with wealth.

Some say Lakshmi has a squint in her eyes so you never know, where she is going or on whom she is bestowing her grace.

Beauty

Lakshmi is always described as beautiful, comely, attractive and alluring. She is even the goddess of cosmetics. Beauty catalyses life-propagating processes. If flowers were not beautiful then pollination and fertilisation cannot take place and they would not turn into fruits. Thus, beauty is considered an essential component of fertility.

Red Saree

Nature is full of energy that transforms into minerals, plants and animals. Red is traditionally the colour of potential energy while green is the colour of realised fertility. Lakshmi as the goddess who represents the beauty and bounty of Nature is therefore visualised draped in red saree.

Sometimes, the goddess of wealth wears a green saree representing the earth when it is covered with a carpet of green vegetation after the rains. Lakshmi in red represents possibilities; Lakshmi in green represents the realization of those possibilities.

Chapter VII

Popular image of Lakshmi found in many Hindu households showing her draped in a red sari and standing on a lotus; modern calendar art.

A bejeweled Lakshmi seated on a lotus that rises from a marsh and holding the pot (symbol of savings) that eternally overflows with grain and gold; modern calendar art.

Fused image of Vishnu (right half of image) and Lakshmi (left half) riding the eagle Garuda. The four arms on the right hold the symbols of *dharma* (from above): discus, conch, mace and lotus while the four arms on the left hold the symbols of *artha* (from above): account book, mirror, lotus and pot; 11th century stone image from Kashmir.

Lakshmi seated on a lotus surrounded by nymphs; Tantrik painting.

Gold Ornaments

Gold is the perfect metal: it never gets polluted, and is extremely malleable and ductile. The goddess Lakshmi therefore adorns herself with gold jewellery. Amongst Hindus, gold is never worn on the foot, unless one is a queen, empress or goddess.

Pot

Lakshmi holds either a pot or a basket in her hand. The pot or basket helps in the collection of Nature's bounty hence is the symbol of wealth. The pot is called the *Akshaya Patra*, the vessel that is never empty. It functions as a cornucopia, eternally overflowing with grain and gold. It is what all devotees seek from Lakshmi.

Lotus

Lakshmi is inseparable from the lotus she sits on and holds in her hands. She is therefore addressed as **Kamala**, **Padma**, or **Padmavati**, which means the lotus-born. The lotus represents the most perfect manifestation of Nature's energy drawn out of a marsh. The goddess

thus embodies the beauty and bounty the material world
has to offer.

White Elephants

Elephants are symbols of royal power. Only kings can
afford to house them. They are also Nature's favourites:
they have no natural enemy, have access to all the
food they want, and because of their size are unstoppable.
Because of their graceful, almost sensuous walk and
love for water they are also associated with fertility.
A white coloured elephant is rare and associated with
auspiciousness and good-luck.

Owl

Lakshmi is often associated with an owl, especially in
East India. Some view the owl as the symbol of
wisdom and luck especially if it is white in colour.
Others view the owl as the symbol of stupidity which
makes man arrogant and foolish when wealth arrives.
The owl is considered a form of Alakshmi, the goddess of
misfortune, who often accompanies her sister.

Invoke O Agni,
the Goddess Lakshmi,
who shines like gold,
yellow in hue, wearing gold
and silver garlands,
blooming like the moon,
the embodiment of wealth.

— *Shri Sukta, Rig Veda*

In Bengal and Orissa, Lakshmi is
shown holding a pot with a conch-
shell (symbol of her father, the god
of oceans) and owl (symbol of her
sister, the goddess of misfortune)
beside her; modern calendar art.

71

Lakshmi at Vishnu's feet; temple wall carving.

Conch-Shell

Conch shells represent the sea, the source of all life, the abode of Lakshmi, the kingdom of her father, Varuna. Right-sided conches are often used to represent Lakshmi and placed beside her image in Bengal and Orissa.

Personality

Lakshmi is fickle, restless, independent, extremely possessive, jealous and easy to displease.

These qualities are often expressed in narratives. Her fickleness is demonstrated by the speed with which she abandons a god or a king in favour of another god or king. She is like the throne or crown of a king, belonging to anyone who sits on the throne and claims the crown. She is attached not to the man but the position.

The only god with whom she has formed a long-lasting relationship is Vishnu probably because he is the embodiment of *dharma*, probably because he keeps taking many incarnations satisfying her restless spirit. As Vishnu's consort she is very jealous and demanding. Vishnu has to constantly work towards keeping her happy. In the process he also domesticates her, a form that is very beneficial to all devotees.

Abode

Lakshmi lives wherever there is water. She is associated with the ocean, the river as well as ponds and marshes, especially those which are fertile enough to let the lotus bloom. Lakshmi's association with water bodies is understandable since water nurtures life. Where there is no water there is no life.

Lakshmi who resides on the chest of Vishnu; cover of a popular music cassette.

Lakshmi is called **Patala-nivasini**, she who lives under the ground. Since plant and mineral wealth emerge from under the ground, it is but natural to associate Lakshmi with the nether regions. Since the nether regions is inhabited by *nagas*, serpents who are guardians of earth's fertility and *asuras*, who are keepers of mineral wealth, Lakshmi is said to reside amongst serpents and demons, before the gods or *devas* who live above the ground pull her out.

In Vaishnava scriptures it is said that Lakshmi resides in Vishnu's heart. Her symbol, a curl of golden hair called Srivatsa, is located on Vishnu's chest. She is also shown seated at Vishnu's feet, demure and domesticated.

Allegorically she is said to reside in the court of kings, in market places, in fields and in banks, wherever wealth and power are generated.

Worship of Lakshmi

Representation

When Lakshmi is worshipped, she is visualised as an independent entity, not as the consort of Vishnu.

Images of Lakshmi seated on a lotus, holding pot overflowing with grain and gold is commonly enshrined in the *pooja* room of most Hindu households.

Lakshmi is sometimes depicted symbolically by placing a brass head of the goddess on a pot filled with water, placed on a pile of rice and topped with a coconut and a coronet of mango leaves.

The goddess is also worshipped in the form of *yantras*, abstract occult diagrams that captures the essential idea of Lakshmi.

Chapter VIII

In most homes the image of Lakshmi is never kept alone as the restless goddess may just slip away. Ganapati is kept beside her as he is the lord of obstacles who prevents her departure. Saraswati is also kept beside her as the goddess of wealth does not like to leave if there is the slightest possibility of the goddess of knowledge getting all the attention.

Lakshmi with the *Shri-kalash*, which is a pot filled with water and topped with a coconut and a coronet of mango leaves; modern greeting card illustration.

Cleanliness and Beauty

An essential part of rituals involving the worship of Lakshmi involves cleaning a place and adorning it with auspicious symbols to attract the benevolent gaze of the goddess.

Before the festival of Diwali, for example, it is mandatory to wash the entire house, repaint the walls, place auspicious symbols around, light incense sticks and decorate the house with leaves and flowers.

Special attention is paid to doorways and thresholds, which are decorated with lamps and flowers.

A woman decorating her house with lamps and mango leaves to attract Lakshmi; modern greeting card illustration.

Games and gambling

Games and gambling are an essential component of Lakshmi worship. Games like card and dice depend on a combinations of luck (the hand one is dealt) and skill. The ritual gambling remind the devotee that Lakshmi's arrival depends on skill and luck, rationality and faith.

The story goes that Shiva and Parvati were playing dice. Shiva asked Vishnu to use his *maya* or power of delusion to make the die turn in his favour. Parvati asked Lakshmi to favour her. With fortune favouring Parvati, no matter how hard Vishnu tried he could not turn the game in Shiva's favour.

Shiva and Parvati playing a game of dice that depends on Lakshmi, goddess of luck; Pahari painting.

Thresholds

The threshold marks the boundary between the wilderness outside and the household inside. All things exist outside. Inside, the householder and housewife seek only good things: fortune, wealth, health, peace and prosperity. Hence, a lot of importance is given to the threshold in Lakshmi worship.

Symbols that draw in forces of fertility and fortune are placed on doorways alongside those that keep out forces of failure and misfortune.

Using rice flour, colour powder and flowers, patterns are drawn near doorways to invite Lakshmi. This is known as *rangoli* in the North, *alpana* in the East and *kolam* in the South. The origin of these patterns seem to be ancient Tantrik *yantras* and *mandalas*, occult diagrams that had the power to attract and harness the wealth of the cosmos.

Rangoli, a floral design made with colour powders in front of the house to attract Lakshmi; photograph.

Pot of Bounty

The *purna-kumbha* or *mangala-kalasha* is symbolic of Lakshmi and the bounty of the world. It is an essential ingredient of all fertility festivals, and ceremonies associated with marriage, childbirth, and joyful occasions. It is never part of ceremonies associated with death.

The *purna-kumbha* is made by decorating a pot with auspicious symbols using turmeric and red *kumkum* powder, placing it on a pile of rice kept on banana leaves. The pot is filled with water, sprouts, sacred flowers and leaves. It is topped with a coconut and a coronet of mango leaves.

Symbolic representation of Lakshmi using a pot, water, coconut, mango leaves and the banana plant; photograph.

75

Lakshmi's Sacred Symbols

 Six-pointed star

 Venus star

 Fly whisk

 Throne

 Lotus

 Shri

 Swastika

 Footprint

 Conch

 Pot

 Diva

 Betel leaf & nut

 Marigold flowers

 Mango leaf

 Sugarcane

 Plantain

 Coconut

 Bilva fruit & leaf

 Grain

 Pile of food

 Basket

 Broom

 Ornaments

 Pearls

 Bejewelled woman

 Fat man

 Mirror

 Kitchen utensils

 Kitchen fire

 Water body

 Cow's footprint

 Honey-comb

 Fish

 Spider

 Lizard

 Cobra

 Elephant

 Cow

 Horse

 Cat

 Capricorn

 Owl

Symbols

The swastika symbol which means *su asti*, let good things happen, is associated with Lakshmi as is the word Shri. This symbol is painted in red in the doorway of houses to invite Lakshmi in.

A pile of rice and sweets expresses the devotees desire for material abundance. Cones of sweets and rice, and even coins, are therefore part of most fertility rituals, especially in South India.

Footprints placed pointing inside the house are said to be *Shri-pada*, the footprint of Lakshmi, bringing in fortune and joy. Another such symbol is *Go-pada*, the footprint of a cow, the animal manifestation of Lakshmi.

Kitchen implements and utensils such as the winnow, broom, frying pan, cooking pot. Ladels and plates are also worshipped as forms of Lakshmi.

Yantra

In *Tantra*, Lakshmi is depicted geometrically through the *Shri Yantra*. This diagram consists of six upward and downward-pointing triangles crisscrossing each other within a lotus.

Upward pointing triangles represent male energy; downward pointing triangles represent female energy. When they intersect each other, they represent the union of male and female principles, hence fertility and creativity. The superimposition of six such unions

Swastika, the symbol which means *su asti*, let good things happen is sacred to Lakshmi and is painted in the house using red kumkum powder.

The Shri *yantra* which is the geometrical representation of Lakshmi in the Tantrik tradition.

Lakshmi letting down a shower of gold after hearing Deshika sing a hymn in her honour; illustration by author.

indicates heightened fertility, which is characteristic of the goddess who embodies cosmic fertility. The lotus within which the triangles are placed represents the cosmos in full bloom charged with the sacred power of Lakshmi.

Other *Yantra*s of Lakshmi include either a schematic six-petalled lotus or a five-pointed pentagram (symbol of the planet Venus) with the word, 'Shri' written in it.

Hymns and Chants

Lakshmi is invoked with a number of hymns such as *Shri Shukta* of the *Rig Veda*, the *Kanakadhara Stotra* composed by Adi Shankaracharya in the 9th century and the *Shri Stuti* composed by Vedanta Deshika in the 13th century.

The story goes that as is expected of students, Shankara went from house to house begging for alms. The lady of one house was so poor that she could give Shankara only a berry. Out of compassion, Shankara composed *Kanakadhara Stotra* praising Lakshmi who was so pleased that she caused a stream (*dhara*) of gold (*kanaka*) berries fall in the courtyard of the poor woman's house.

A similar story is told of Deshika. A poor man asked him for money so that he could get married. Deshika was poor himself but did not want to turn the man away. So he composed the *Shri Stuti* in praise of Lakshmi. As a result there was a shower of gold coins much to the delight of the young man. Deshika was so detached that he turned away without even looking at a single coin.

Sacred Plants

The coconut, banana, mango, marigold, Tulsi and Bilva plants are associated with Lakshmi.

The coconut is the perfect manifestation of Nature's benevolence. It does not need to be farmed; it grows on its own. Each part of the palm can be put to some economic use.

The banana plant is also of great economic value. Hindus use its leaves as plates during feasts. Its fruits are extremely sweet and nourishing. The trunk is often used to make rafts. When the stem is cut, the plant regenerates itself making it worthy of adoration.

The mango's sweetness and its flowering in spring has led to its association with Manmatha, the god of love, son of Lakshmi. The marigold flower whose petals

A woman placing lamps in the courtyard of her house next to the Tulsi plant; modern greeting card illustration.

A doorway in Rajasthan decorated with the sacred image of Lakshmi and her white elephants; photograph.

Doorway decorated with marigold flowers, mango leaves, sugarcane, banana plant and *rangoli* to attract Lakshmi; illustration by author.

contain seeds is also considered a symbol of Manmatha as it is highly fertile. Both, the mango leaf and the marigold flower are strung up as garlands across doorways on auspicious days to entice Lakshmi into the house.

Lakshmi is associated with the Tulsi plant. No worship to Vishnu is complete without an offering of Tulsi springs. In Vaishnava households, this plant is grown in the courtyard, worshipped every day, and after the rains, following Diwali, this plant is ritually given in marriage to Vishnu. In some narratives, Tulsi is seen as Lakshmi's co-wife (either Radha or the goddess Vrinda) of whom the goddess is extremely jealous, but who represents unconditional devotion. Lakshmi resides in the house with Vishnu but Tulsi is kept out in the courtyard.

Lakshmi is also associated with the Bilva fruit. The story goes that Lakshmi once promised to make an offering of thousand lotuses to Shiva. To test her devotion, Shiva hid one of the thousand lotuses she had gathered. When Lakshmi discovered she was one lotus short, she went round the world looking for a lotus but found none. Determined to fulfill her promise to Shiva, she cut one of her breasts that had been described by poets as the breast of a lotus flower and offered it to Shiva. Pleased by this display of devotion,

Lakshmi riding white elephants that represent divinity, royal power, strength, unstoppability and fertility; modern calendar art.

The river-goddesses Ganga riding the elephant-headed fish or dolphin called *makara* (left) and Yamuna riding a turtle (right); 10th century stone carvings from North India.

Shiva transformed Lakshmi's breast into the Bilva fruit and declared that the Bilva fruit and Bilva leaves would be an integral part of his worship.

Betel nut and betel leaves are chewed in contentment and joy, hence are symbols of worldly life and sacred to Lakshmi.

Sacred Animals

Lakshmi is associated with all animals that offer material benefit such as the cow and represent earthly power such as the horse and elephant.

The cow provides milk and dung that serves as food and fuel to most Hindus. It is therefore sacred to Lakshmi. Cow is viewed as a symbol of the earth-goddess. Just as the cow must be tended with care and milked with love, so must the earth be respected and its bounty drawn with care.

The elephant is associated with fertility and the horse with virility. Hence both animals are sacred to Lakshmi. Since Lakshmi is born in the realm of *asura*s and rises to the realm of *deva*s, Brihaspati, the *guru* of *deva*s, is associated with an elephant while Shukra, the guru of *asura*s, is linked to a horse.

In eastern parts of India, the goddess is associated with white owls. There are many reasons for this. The owl is considered a wise bird. It eats rodents and other pests. This makes the bird sacred. Some scholars believe the owl

Bilva leaves offered to Shiva are symbols of Lakshmi and embodiments of devotion; illustration by author.

81

Lakshmi wearing an elaborate nose-ring and other gold ornaments indicating her rootedness and marriage to the household; photograph.

represents Alakshmi, the goddess of misfortune, who has been defeated and subjugated by Lakshmi.

The fish represents the abundance of the water. It is also never still, like wealth, constantly on the move and hence is considered a fertility symbol. The *makara*, a mythical creature that is part fish, part elephant and part goat, is sacred to Manmatha, the son of Lakshmi. Vishnu wears *makara*-shaped earrings. This beast is a fertility symbol too. Turtle, another aquatic animal, symbol of stability and an incarnation of Vishnu, is also associated with Lakshmi.

The river-goddess **Ganga** rides a *makara* while the river-goddess **Yamuna** rides a turtle. Both these river-goddesses are considered manifestations of Lakshmi as they nurture life wherever they go.

Lakshmi is also associated with spiders, which are symbols of hardwork and homemaking activities like spinning. In many parts of India, lizards are worshipped as the symbol of Lakshmi probably because they eat cockroaches which are household pests. In Kanchipuram in Tamil Nadu, the image of the golden lizard on the roof of the temple of the goddess Kamakshi is touched by devotees as it is believed to bring good luck. Cats are also sacred to Lakshmi because female cats are fertile and fiercely protective of their young.

Sacred Minerals

As the goddess of wealth, Lakshmi is associated with all minerals and gems. But she is particularly associated with gold, the most perfect of minerals, and diamonds, the most perfect of gems.

Pearls are also considered sacred because they are associated with the sea, the source of all water. Conch-shells, another marine product, is sacred to Lakshmi especially if they open to the right side (which is rare).

Out of deference to Lakshmi gold and diamonds are never used to make ornaments for the feet such as toe rings and anklets.

Sacred Days

Lakshmi is commonly worshipped on Thursday or Friday. On these days women perform *vrata* to invoke the goddess and obtain her blessings. Women fast, make offerings to the goddess, stay up all night thinking of her, chanting her names and singing her praises.

Thursday is associated with Brihaspati, the *guru* of *devas*, lord of the planet Jupiter, overseer of rational thought. Friday is associated with Shukra, the *guru* of *asuras*, lord

A *yaksha* blowing a conch which is sacred to Lakshmi; temple wall carving from South India.

of the planet Venus, overseer of intuitive and creative thought.

Since Lakshmi lives in the subterranean realm of *asura*s and acquires value when she moves to the realm of *deva*s above ground, worshipping Lakshmi on days associated with Brihaspati and Shukra makes logical sense.

Lakshmi, Shukra, Venus and Friday

All cultures have given great importance to fertility of plants and animals. Prosperity of any society depends on good harvests and the multiplication of farm animals. It is interesting that the symbols, days and deities associated with fertility share similar traits all over the world. The relationship of Friday with the planet Venus (Shukra in Sanskrit) and Lakshmi is a case in point.

Lakshmi is worshipped on Friday, the day that is sacred to Shukra, the guru of *asura*s. Shukra's father Bhrigu, one of the seven primal sons of Brahma, is also Lakshmi's father as indicated by her name Bhargavi. This makes Shukra Lakshmi's brother.

The root of the word 'Friday' comes from Freia, the Viking goddess of fertility. She was associated with the planet called Venus (known in Hindu astrology as Shukra). Venus was the Roman goddess of fertility. Her Greek counterpart was known as Aphrodite. Hindus saw Venus in male form as Shukra and referred to Friday as the day of Venus, *Shukra-vaar*. Thus, as in all ancient cultures, Hindus found a common thread between Friday, the planet Venus and the worship of deities associated with fertility.

Venus, the Greco-Roman goddess of fertility and love, rising from the sea in a conch-shell, just like Lakshmi.

The word 'Friday' owes its origin to Freia or Freyja, the ancient goddess of fertility and childbirth in the Viking tradition. Like Lakshmi, this goddess was closely associated with cats because female cats are known for their fertility and maternal affection.

A statue-maker making images of Lakshmi that will be enshrined and worshipped by devotees on festivals; photograph.

Like the Hindu goddess of fertility Lakshmi, Aphrodite and Venus emerged from the sea. Consequently, marine products like conch and pearls are an integral part of their worship. The son of all three goddesses is the god of love who catalyses the process of fertilisation. Hindus know him as Manmatha or Kama, Greeks knew him as Eros and Romans as Cupid.

In epics, Shukra is said to have two daughters: Ara and Devayani. Dandaka raped Ara while Yayati was unfaithful to Devayani. Shukra cursed these two men. Dandaka's kingdom became desolate and transformed into an inhospitable forest called Dandakaranya. Yayati became old and impotent. Shukra may be seen as the guardian of Lakshmi, his sister and daughter. Anyone who hurts her incurs his wrath.

Obese Forms

Image of happy-looking fat moustached men with their bejewelled plump wives adorn Hindu, Jain and Buddhist shrines. These *yaksha-murti*s represent household fulfilment, contentment and prosperity. Such images are considered good luck charms. They represent what Lakshmi can offer and are symbolically made part of household rituals.

Offerings

Lakshmi is offered lotus flowers, sweet food and bridal finery especially nose rings.

Offering of bridal finery indicates the desire to see the goddess in her domesticated form, not as a wild forest but as a field that offers economic benefits and does not threaten the well being of man.

The goddess is offered sweet food cooked with butter and jaggery inside the house. Offerings of sour and pungent food like lemon and chillies are kept outside the house to satisfy the hunger of her unwanted sister, Alakshmi, the goddess of misfortune.

A pair of happy and obese *yaksha-murti*s are considered good luck charms; photograph.

Festivals of Lakshmi

Chapter IX

Nava-ratri

In autumn, following four months of the monsoon rains, the mother-goddess is invoked in her nine forms through the nine nights known as *Nava-ratri*. It is said that during these days the goddess as **Durga** battled the buffalo-demon. On the final day known as *Dussera* or *Vijayadashami*, her victory is commemorated.

In Bengal, Durga is worshipped along with her two daughters, Lakshmi and Saraswati, and her sons, Ganapati and Kartikeya. She is welcomed as the daughter returning to her mother's house after marriage. Together, they bring into the household a balance between wealth (Lakshmi) and knowledge (Saraswati), brain (Ganapati) and brawn (Kartikeya).

In South India, during *Nava-ratri*, the goddess is worshipped for three nights as Lakshmi, three nights as Saraswati and three nights as Kali. According to one legend, the goddess stood on a point of a needle and did *tapas* for nine nights transforming from the fierce *tamasic* Kali to the ravishing *rajasic* Lakshmi and finally into the serene *sattvic* Saraswati.

In Gujarat, women sing, bend, clap, sway and dance in circles the dance known as *garba* (meaning womb) which celebrates the fertility of Bhoo-devi, the earth.

In Bengal, during the festival of Dussera, the goddess Durga who kills the buffalo-demon Mahisha is worshipped. Lakshmi (left) and Saraswati (right) are said to be her daughters; photograph.

Women gathering to celebrate *Kojagiri* or *Sharad Poornima* when Lakshmi rises and takes the form of Radha to dance with Krishna; North Indian miniature painting.

Lakshmi rises from her sleep in the autumn full moon; temple wall carving from South India.

Sharad Poornima (Kojagiri)

It is said that the mother-goddess acquires a fierce form during her battle with the buffalo-demon through *Navaratri*. After the battle, which culminates on *Vijayadashami*, she rests, sheds her rage and awakens as the resplendent Lakshmi on *Sharad Poornima* night.

This is the full moon night between *Dussera* and *Diwali* that falls in October or November, when the autumn moon illuminates the earth through the night. On this night, Lakshmi takes the form of Radha and dances the *rasa-leela* with Krishna. He plays the flute and she dances in a circle around him.

This night is known as *Kojagiri*, which literally means, "Who wakes up." Devotees are told to fast and stay up all night to welcome the goddess of wealth and fortune. In temples, drums are beaten in joyful anticipation.

In Bengal and Orissa, special *pooja* is held to welcome Lakshmi whose image is enshrined in pandals. In other parts of India, especially in the North, people wait for a fortnight and welcome the goddess of wealth on Diwali.

Diwali

Diwali or *Deepawali*, the festival of light, is the most popular festival of Lakshmi, which is celebrated over five nights around the new moon night that follows *Sharad Poornima*. On these nights, devotees light lamps, burst crackers, burn incense and distribute sweets. The light, sound, fragrance and flavour is supposed to drive out forces of misfortune and attract forces of fortune. The five days are:

Dhanteras or *Dhan Trayodashi*: thirteenth day of the waning moon, when gold, silver, utensils and anything metallic are purchased and brought to the house, believing them to be tangible manifestations of Lakshmi.

Naraka Chaturdashi: fourteenth day of the waning moon, to celebrate the liberation by Krishna of the world's wealth stolen by the demon Naraka. Also known as *Kali Choudas*, on this day the thirst of Kali, the wild form of the goddess, is quenched so that she transforms into the domestic Lakshmi.

Lakshmi Pujan (Amavasya): the new moon night, to celebrate the rise of Lakshmi from the ocean of milk and the rise of the *asura*-king Bali from the nether regions. On this night, the sun enters the House of Libra. Since the constellation Libra is like a balance, on this day Hindu traders balance their books and open new account books. Gold purchased on *Dhanteras* is placed beside the image of Lakshmi (usually embossed on gold or silver coins) worshipped on this day.

Bali Pratipada: the first day of the waxing moon, when Vishnu shoves Bali back to his subterranean realm. *Annakoota* is celebrated in North Indian temples. Vast amounts of food, usually rice and sugar balls, are piled up in the shape of a mountain to celebrate the bounty of earth.

Lakshmi-*deepa*, the lamp of Lakshmi that is popular in South India; photograph.

A woman putting *rangoli* to attract Lakshmi on the nights of Diwali; modern greeting card illustration.

Lakshmi is worshipped along with money and gold coins on the new moon night of Diwali when traders and businessmen of North India open new account books.

Yama Dvitiya: the second day of the waxing moon, when brothers visit their sisters and reinforce sibling love with gifts. Women are considered diminutive doubles of Lakshmi. Since they leave the house after marriage, an annual trip to her house by the brother is an acknowledgment of Lakshmi who was given away to another household.

During Diwali the house is cleaned and threshold decorated with bright designs and auspicious symbols. Mango leaves and marigold flowers are strung along the doorway. Mango and marigold is associated with Manmatha, the god of love, the son of Lakshmi.

Women lighting lamps to attract Lakshmi who rises from the ocean of milk on Diwali; modern greeting card illustration.

The *rangoli*, known as *kolam* in the South and *alpana* in the East, is a design made just outside the main doorway of the house with coloured powder or rice paste. It is an integral part of celebrations, as is the *kandil* or lantern hung high above the house. Oil lamps are placed along verandahs and corridors.

People gamble on this day using card and dice to realize the fickleness of fortune. Success on these games depends partly on luck and partly on skill. One has no control over luck. But one does have control over skill. Thus by playing these games, devotees realise that with an interplay of luck, which is the grace of Lakshmi, and skill, which is in our hands, we can acquire worldly riches.

88

Vara-Lakshmi Vrata

On the Friday that precedes the full moon night of *Shravan* (September-October), south Indian women perform the Vara-Lakshmi *Pooja*. It involves invoking the goddess of boons, Vara-Lakshmi, and seeking from her: *Dhan* (wealth), *Dhanya* (food), *Sampatti* (property), *Arogya* (health), *Santan* (children), *Saumangalya* (well being of the husband), *Sukha* (happiness) and *Shanti* (peace).

Early in the morning women dressed in bridal finery place on a pile of rice a pot filled with water, rice, sprouts, gold, turmeric, areca nut, betel leaves. On the pot is placed a turmeric-smeared coconut (sometimes topped with a metal face of the goddess) with a coronet of mango leaves. The story of the *vrata*, how performing it helped many people, is read out. 108 names of the goddess are chanted. She is praised and her blessings are sought by those assembled. No one is allowed to get up until the ritual is complete for fear of annoying the impatient, demanding and restless goddess.

Image worshipped during Vara-Lakshmi *vrata*, which is performed in South India by housewives to invoke the grace of the goddess of wealth and fortune; photograph.

Vishu and Onam

Vishu (known as Baisakhi in the North) and Onam are harvest festivals of Kerala.

On the morning of Vishu, the first thing all members of the household are encouraged to see is a collection of Lakshmi's symbols: mirror, grain, gold, fruits, vegetables, water and flowers.

Onam commemorates the rise of the *asura*-king Bali from the subterranean region. With him comes the harvest and prosperity. Although not directly linked with the worship of Lakshmi, it shows the close association of prosperity, hence Lakshmi, with *asura*s.

Women in Kerala dancing around floral *rangoli*s during Onam to welcome the *asura*-king Bali; photograph.

Mahalakshmi of Kolhapur,
Maharashtra, is considered a fierce
manifestation of Lakshmi and is
more associated with Durga; prayer
book cover.

Temples of Lakshmi

Though Lakshmi is an extremely popular goddess and her image can be found in most Hindu homes and business establishments, there are very few temples dedicated solely to Lakshmi.

Lakshmi temples usually form part of temple complexes dedicated to Vishnu where she is enshrined as the consort of the patron deity. Thus Lakshmi temples are located within the temple complex dedicated to Jagannath in Puri, Orissa; Varadaraja in Kanchi, Tamil Nadu; and Ranganatha, in Srirangam, Tamil Nadu. The reason for this lies in the belief that an independent Lakshmi is restless and does not stay in one place; seated beside Vishnu she remains rooted to the temple. In rituals, there are often mock quarrels between Vishnu and Lakshmi. As a result, their respective images though within one complex are not located under the same roof.

Now-a-days, temples are being built dedicated only to Lakshmi. In Hyderabad and Chennai are *Ashta*-Lakshmi temples enshrining the eight forms of Lakshmi bestowing the eight most sought-after gifts of life. These were built less than 30 years ago. Architecturally, they are unique and quite modern. The Hyderabad temple for example has the eight forms of the goddess arranged in a circle and a ninth form with Vishnu at the centre.

In Maharashtra, Maha-Lakshmi temples do exist. But the Maha-Lakshmi referred to is not Lakshmi, the goddess of wealth. It is the supreme mother-goddess **Adi-Maya-Shakti**. This form of the goddess is fierce and wild, not demure or domestic. In these temples, Lakshmi is associated with the lion indicating she is less the goddess of wealth and more the goddess of war, Durga, who bestows royal power to kings. Locally, Maha-Lakshmi is known simply as 'Amba' or mother.

Maha-Lakshmi Temple in Kolhapur

Sage Bhrigu once visited Vaikuntha. Vishnu who was reclining on his couch did not see him. Angry at being ignored the sage kicked Vishnu on the chest. Rather than getting upset, Vishnu apologized for not acknowledging the sage and hoped that his foot did not hurt too much after the kick. Vishnu's humility angered Lakshmi. She expected him to strike the sage for kicking his heart, the abode of Lakshmi. In her rage, she abandoned Vaikuntha. Vishnu followed her to earth and tracked her to Karavirapura, the ancient name of Kolhapur. She was too angry to return.

Chapter X

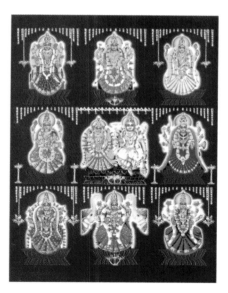

The eight forms of Lakshmi that are worshipped at the modern *Ashta*-Lakshmi temple in Hyderabad, Andhra Pradesh; temple sticker.

Bhrigu kicking the chest of Vishnu which happens to be the abode of Lakshmi; comic book illustration.

Vishnu took the form of Venkateshwara, presiding deity of Tirupati, in order to woo the angry Lakshmi back to Vaikuntha. She resides in Kolhapur; photograph.

Until Lakshmi calms down and agrees to return, Vishnu has chosen to stay on the hills of Tirumalai as Venkateshwara Balaji. On the foothills of Tirumalai, at Tiruchanur, stands the temple of Padmavati, the local consort of Venkateshwara. She was the princess of the king who ruled the hill. Only after marrying her did he receive permission to reside atop the hill. The name of the princess (Padmavati, the lotus-born), her worship according to *Pancharatra* rites, and her independent spirit expressed by her temple's location at the foot of the hill, indicates that she is a manifestation of Lakshmi.

In fact, in many parts of Andhra Pradesh and Tamil Nadu, there are temples enshrining local goddesses who are identified with Lakshmi. Near Kumbhakonam, in Tamil Nadu at Tirunaraiyur, is the temple of Vanjulavalli. The goddess is considered to be Lakshmi who left Vaikuntha after a quarrel with Vishnu. She manifested as a girl under a *vanjula* or *ashoka* tree, was raised by a priest called Medhavi, a manifestation of Bhrigu. Vishnu fell in love with Vanjulavalli and agreed to stay there with her. Medhavi insisted that in all temple rituals his daughter not son-in-law must get prime importance.

South Indian temple image of Vishnu flanked by his two consorts, the two forms of Lakshmi: Shridevi and Bhoodevi.

At Kolhapur, the image of the goddess, locally known as **Karavir-vasini** Devi, is associated with a hooded serpent, a lion and the *linga* of Shiva, indicating she is more likely to be a *Grama*-devi, village-goddess, a parochial manifestation of Shakti, the primal mother-goddess, rather than the goddess of wealth. The image, unlike in most shrines, faces the west instead of the traditional east or north. Twice a year the rays of the setting sun fall on the face of the goddess through a hole in the western wall. On these days (21st of March and September), hundreds gather to witness this spectacle. Interestingly, west is the direction ruled by Varuna, god of the sea, Lakshmi's father.

92

Maha-Lakshmi Temple in Mumbai

In Maha-Lakshmi temple in the city of Mumbai, Lakshmi is worshipped along with Saraswati and Kali. Together they make up the three aspects of the supreme mother-goddess representing bounty, wisdom and strength. The absence of any image of Vishnu and the presence of a lion before the shrine indicates that the presiding deity of the temple is not the domestic goddess of wealth, rather the independent goddess Adi-Maya-Shakti who embodies the whole world.

It is said that in the 1890s, when the adjoining causeway was being constructed by a British engineer, the project was always jinxed: every time the foundation was laid, the sea would rush in and destroy it. Then one night, a labourer dreamt of Lakshmi who ordered him to dig out an idol from a spot under the causeway and build a shrine on it. This was done, and the causeway was ultimately completed.

Mahalakshmi temple in Mumbai enshrines the images of the three forms of the mother-goddess, (from right) Saraswati, Lakshmi and Kali who are fountainheads of knowledge, wealth and strength; photograph.

Lakshmi sitting on the lap of
Vishnu and providing him with the
wherewithal to sustain the cosmos.
Vishnu's mount, the eagle Garuda,
holds a pot of *amrita* (elixir of
youthfulness), binds serpents
(symbols of renewal) and looks like a
parrot (symbol of love); Pahari
painting.

Relevance of Lakshmi

Does one have to give up wealth to find God? Must one abandon all earthly pleasures to be spiritual? If yes, why do Hindus visualize wealth as a goddess and consider prosperity a manifestation of divine grace?

Understanding the mythology of Lakshmi — her narratives, symbols and rituals — helps in understanding the true nature of wealth. A materialism emerging from such an understanding is in fact no different from spiritualism.

Foundation of Life

Hindu scriptures say that the purpose of life is to understand who we really are. We cannot discover this until we experience life. To experience life, we must live. To live, we need to nourish ourselves. Lakshmi is source of all nourishment.

Lakshmi, the bestower of affluence, abundance and auspiciousness; modern greeting card illustration.

95

Water is poured on images of Shiva to symbolically request the divine hermit to transfer his ascetic power to worldly life; Pahari miniature.

Lakshmi embodies the abundance of the universe, the boundless bounty of the cosmos. Seated on a thousand-petalled dew-drenched lotus that rises from the ocean of milk, flanked by trumpeting white elephants, entertained by buzzing bees and chirping parrots, surrounded by nymphs and musicians, draped in red sari, resplendent with every jewel imaginable, with a fragrant pollen-rich garland round her neck, she smiles affectionately and showers the wealth of the cosmos that sustains all living creatures.

It comes as no surprise then that Lakshmi is represented by water. Where there is water there is life. A civilization, however great, will collapse in drought.

In Hindu mythology, drought is often linked with ascetic practices. The hermit-god Shiva is associated with barren surroundings like icy mountains. His withdrawal from worldly life is considered sterile. In folk songs he is chastised for his inability to please his spouse or provide for his children. Water is poured on him and he is requested by the gods to adorn himself with silks, flowers and jewels: make himself more appealing and less distant to his worldly devotees. Thus, in the Hindu scheme of things, there is an overall appreciation of wealth as an essential ingredient of worldly life. So much so that displays of wealth are integral to household rituals. They are not only celebrations of earthly life but also symbols of auspiciousness!

Enchanting yet Ephemeral

Water, the symbol of Lakshmi, is known as *apsa* in Sanskrit. From this term, comes the word *apsara* meaning 'water-nymph'. *Apsara*s are handmaidens of Lakshmi. They rose from the ocean of milk along with the goddess of wealth. They represent the material joys of life. And like all things material, they are enchanting and ephemeral.

Balarama uses his plough to divert the flow of the river-goddess Yamuna symbolizing how mankind harnesses the life-bestowing power of rivers in agriculture; Pahari miniature.

The conflict between the ways of the householder and the hermit is represented on temple walls by the water-nymph and the fire-hermit; temple wall carving from Gujarat.

The hermit sees material things as the root of all sorrow and turns away from it. The householder sees material things as the root of all happiness and runs after it.
In narratives, the *apsara* seduces the hermit and eludes the householder, causing both to suffer. This is because neither appreciates the true nature of worldly wealth. The hermit has to realize that wealth is essential to life — one cannot turn one's back on it. The householder has to realize that wealth is transitory — it will slip away like water from a clenched fist.

The ritual of fasting helps devotees appreciate how vital Lakshmi is for existence. The riverside ritual of collecting water in the palms of our hands and then pouring it back reminds devotees that wealth taken from the cosmos eventually returns to it.

Man pouring water collected in his palms back into river so as to ritually acknowledge the cycle of life and wealth from nature to culture and back; modern illustration.

The Restless One

Water must flow otherwise it will stagnate and breed diseases. Food must be consumed or distributed otherwise it will rot. In the same way, wealth must flow so that it can nourish society. For the economy to thrive, wealth needs to be constantly created and distributed. Lakshmi enriches and empowers only when she is in motion. Hence she is known as the restless one, Chanchala. She needs to always be on the move. Any attempt to pin her down and hoard her earns her wrath.

97

*Asura*s are killed to release the wealth they hoard. But they are also necessary for regeneration of wealth as they possess the secret of renewal known as *Sanjivani vidya*, hence defeat of demons is never final — after one is killed, another rises; wood carving from Orissa.

To churn Lakshmi out of the ocean of milk, Vishnu (god who maintains universal stability) takes the help of *deva*s and *asura*s who represent the forces of wealth distribution and wealth regneration; temple wall carving from Angkor Wat in Cambodia.

This is why all harvest festivals, such as Dussera and Diwali, are associated with tales of gods defeating *asura*s: Durga kills Mahisha, Rama kills Ravana, Vamana crushes Bali, and Krishna kills Naraka. *Asura*s, as residents of the nether regions and keepers of the science of rejuvenation known as *Sanjivani vidya*, constantly restore earth's fertility and mineral deposits. They create wealth but do not distribute it. Gods release the hoarded wealth by force after defeating them in battle.

During Diwali, gifts are given liberally to ensure wealth exchanges hands. Utensils and jewellery are displayed for all to see and admire. Food is shared. There is a celebration of the inflow of wealth and a symbolic rejection of hoarding.

Without any Favourites

After defeating *asura*s, the *deva*s take the spoils of war to their heavenly abode where they live a life of abundance and affluence. All their needs are met by the wish-fulfilling tree Kalpataru, a dream-realizing cow Kamadhenu and a desire-fulfilling gem called Chintamani. But when Indra, king of the gods, overindulges in wine and the company of nymphs, he incurs the wrath of sages who curse him with poverty and misfortune. Lakshmi departs from his side instantly. That the king of the gods can also lose his wealth reminds us that Lakshmi is attached to no one. She stays so long as she is treated with reverence and her value is realized. She turns her back on those who are unworthy of her affection.

Lakshmi has no favourites. She does not discriminate on the basis of caste, gender, creed, or social status. The same bowl of rice can satisfy the hunger of a king and a beggar, the same blanket will provide warmth to a man or a eunuch, the same roof will shelter equally the judge and the criminal. She will go to anyone who seeks her and makes himself worthy of her.

Shrinathji of Nathdvara as half Krishna (Vishnu) and half Radha (Lakshmi) symbolizing how order and prosperity depend on each other. With stability comes prosperity, with poverty comes instability; modern calendar art.

Lakshmi makes no moral judgements. This idea is driven home by descriptions of Ravana and Duryodhana – villians of the Hindu epics *Ramayana* and *Mahabharata* — as affluent monarchs. Ravana lived in a city of gold while the hero-god Rama lived like a hermit in the forest for 14 years. The unrighteous Duryodhana always lived as a king in Hastinapur while the righteous Yudhishtira was born in a forest and spent much of his life in exile or in hiding.

Wealth and power are essentially impersonal. They come with a position not a person. People bow not to the man under the crown but to the crown itself. The symbols of kingship — crown, umbrella, throne, footstool, flywhisk, banners and scepter — remind us that our wealth and our power are not dependent on us. We need wealth and power, wealth and power does not need us. When the rich man dies, his wealth outlives him sustaining all those who are left behind. When the powerful man dies, the power he yielded goes to someone as worthy or gets distributed amongst many.

The spiritual man therefore does not get carried away by the bounty of Lakshmi. He knows that she will stay with him only as long as he makes himself worthy of her. If he fails to keep her, she will leave him.

Indra, king of the *deva*s, cannot hold on to Lakshmi for long as he invariably overindulges in women and wine and ignores his *dharma*; temple wall carving from Orissa.

99

Consort of Order

Even though Lakshmi is said to be whimsical and restless, she is the eternal consort of Vishnu. She sits demurely at his feet and serves him devotedly.

Vishnu is the sustainer of the cosmos who institutes the code of *dharma*. This code demands that all creatures do their duty and live disciplined lives. Vishnu's *dharma* ensures there is rhythm in Nature and order in culture. The discus whirling round Vishnu's finger indicates stability. When *dharma* is ignored, Vishnu blows his conch and strikes down troublemakers with his mace.

Vishnu knows that his strength comes from Lakshmi. He therefore keeps Lakshmi in his heart. This earns him the title of 'Shrivatsal' — the abode of the goddess of wealth. Just as the kingdom gives a king his power and in return, the king makes sure the kingdom is secure and prosperous, there is a mutual interdependence between Vishnu and Lakshmi.

The association of Lakshmi with Vishnu drives home the idea that pleasure, prosperity and power come wherever there is peace and stability. In Hinduism, lamps represent *dharma*. Just as a lamp drives away darkness, *dharma* drives away anarchy and ignorance. By lighting lamps, devotees symbolically embrace *dharma*. Since Lakshmi is attracted to *dharma*, she is said to favour households where lamps are lit every night.

A Sister called Strife

With wealth comes power. With power comes pride and arrogance. Wealth can make people around jealous. Wealth and power are often at the root of quarrels and discontentment. This is why Lakshmi is said to have a sister called Alakshmi, the goddess of discord and misfortune. To remind us of her presence, she is represented by an owl and placed next to Lakshmi's image.

Narratives and hymns describe her as Jyestha, the elder sister, and as being dear to Lakshmi. One is advised to respect her and take cognizance of her presence. A devotee of Lakshmi ignores Alakshmi at his peril. For when the elder sister is not acknowledged, she makes her presence felt by filling the house with stress and strife.

A spiritual man knows that Alakshmi always accompanies Lakshmi. Sensitive to the havoc she can wreak, he is constantly vigilant. He does everything in his power to keep her away — he keeps his body and his vicinity clean and beautiful, he shuns sloth and indiscipline, and he constantly chants, "Lakshmi looks beautiful when she enters the house, Alakshmi looks beautiful when she leaves the house."

Saraswati, the goddess of knowledge, who prevents Alakshmi, the goddess of strife and stupidity, from accompanying her sister Lakshmi, the goddess of wealth.

Lakshmi with the owl who represents her sister Alakshmi, the goddess of strife, who accompanies wealth and prosperity and can create trouble if not given due attention; modern calendar art.

Gentler Face of God

According to Hindus, man has four goals in life: *dharma* (social obligations), *artha* (economic and political achievements), *kama* (pleasurable pursuits) and *moksha* (spiritual liberation). Lakshmi is the consort of the god who embodies *dharma*, she is the mother of the god who patronizes *kama* and catalyzes *artha*. She is also the medium for *moksha*.

How is it that the goddess who showers the delights of material life, also grants the means for spiritual liberation? The answers are given by the *Shri Vaishnava* school of devotion which is widespread in South India.

According to this school, Vishnu is the creator, sustainer and destroyer of the world. Only he can grant living beings liberation from material existence. Only by submitting oneself to Vishnu can man break free from the fetters of worldly life.

But Vishnu is a rather stern and aloof divinity. His awesome and transcendent nature makes him all but unapproachable to the lowly devotee.

Lakshmi, Vishnu's cherished consort, provides an aspect of the divine that is far more intimate and tender. She appeals to Vishnu for the devotee's welfare, like a loving mother mediating between father and son.

Vishnu gently embracing Lakshmi while she pleads on behalf of mankind; temple wall carving from Khajuraho, Madhya Pradesh.

Vishnu as Jagannath, lord of the world, who is worshipped in Puri, Orissa. He is said to have two wives, Lakshmi and Saraswati, who give him wealth and knowledge to institute and maintain order; modern calendar art.

When man does not live according to *dharma*, Vishnu seeks to punish man. But Lakshmi pleads, "If you punish him, instead of saving him, your quality of grace will not survive." Elsewhere, she softens Vishnu's stern heart with her charm and forces him to grant salvation to the devotee.

Quarrels with Saraswati

Lakshmi and Saraswati are sometimes viewed as the co-wives of Vishnu. He needs them both to sustain the universe. But they always fight. The relationship of Lakshmi and Saraswati remind us of the tension between wealth and knowledge. We need them both. Without one we can never realize the value of the other. The truly spiritual man worships Lakshmi with Saraswati for without Saraswati, wealth has no meaning and brings with it arrogance, discontentment and strife. Saraswati stabilizes Lakshmi — an enlightened mind knows how not to get swept away by the wonders of worldly life.

Lakshmi's Father

The sea-god Varuna is called Lakshmi's father. This is understandable because the sea is the ultimate source of water, hence life. It is also a boundless source of wealth. The wealth of the sea — salt, coconuts, pearls, corals, fish, water — has to be simply harvested; no cultivation is required. The waves keep giving and take nothing in return. Thus Lakshmi's father is infinitely wealthy and boundlessly selfless. The rising and ebbing tide reminds us that fortune comes and goes in cycles, and that misfortune is never permanent.

A truly spiritual man is like the sea — constantly working towards the generation and redistribution of wealth, which he views as the force that nourishes, enriches and empowers everything. He knows that it is foolhardy to ignore, crave or hoard wealth and futile to clog channels through which it flows. The movement Lakshmi sustains civilization and rotates the cycle of life. What is given out comes back eventually, just as water evaporating into the clouds flows backs into the sea as rain and river.

Mother of Pleasure and Prosperity

When Lakshmi arrives, there is joy. It is like finding an oasis in a desert or watching rain fall after a long spell of drought. Plants sing, animals dance. Lakshmi not only sustains life, she also makes life enjoyable. When Lakshmi disappears there is hunger, barrenness and gloom. Even the gods are helpless and miserable. This is why she is known as the mother of Kandarpa, lord of delight, also known as Manmatha or Kama-deva.

Varuna, the god of sea, father of Lakshmi, symbol of selfless generosity; temple carving from Orissa.

Saraswati, goddess of knowledge; Patta painting from Orissa.

Kandarpa rides a parrot, and shoots flowery darts with his sugarcane bow to rouse the five senses. He makes life thrilling and exciting, showering existence with colour, fragrance, music, desire and love.

Kandarpa unites the bee and the flower, the man and the woman, the seed and the soil. He brings the bull to the cow, the gander to the goose, the stag to the doe. The result is new life — more children, a better harvest, a larger herd. In other words, there is fertility, prosperity, growth. This is why symbols of Lakshmi's son — sugarcane, parrots, mango leaves, marigold flowers, honey and butterflies — represent joy as well as fertility, sensual pleasures (*kama*) as well as economic growth (*artha*). They form an integral part of household rituals that seek to harness the abundance of the cosmos.

When death happens, pots are broken and food is not cooked in the Hindu household as a sign of mourning. After the period of bereavement, the house is decorated with life-affirming symbols of Lakshmi and her son. Red colour *swastika*s are painted on the doorway, mango leaves are strung along with marigold flowers on the threshold, water pots topped with a coconut and coronet of mango leaves are placed on heaps of rice, lamps are lit, incense burnt, food cooked, betel nuts offered and music played.

Lakshmi fills our life with the wonders of the cosmos. Her delightful gifts make us look towards the source — towards God. To her is dedicated this prayer.

Manmatha, Kandarpa or Kama-deva, the god of pleasure, fertility, love and lust, who is the son of Lakshmi; Tanjore painting.

> *I meditate upon a still pool surrounded by mountains*
> *And in its center is a clear full moon*
> *Shimmering in golden rays outward are her manifestations*
> *Spinning the skies crazily, making the stars dance*
> *To her ancient rhythms.*
>
> *O Lakshmi, mother of divine grace*
> *Source of sacred energy and infinite bliss*
> *I worship you and your sacred spouse*
> *Hari, the essence of sweet nectar*
> *Which is your true nature.*
>
> *Lady of luck, lady of bliss*
> *You are the goddess to whom I offer all*
> *I gamble my heart and soul on the hope*
> *That you will hear me.*
>
> *May I embody your essence as Fortune,*
> *As luck, and engenderer of new beginnings.*
>
> *May I be sure-footed upon the circling wheels of Time*
> *Skipping rocks of joy and sorrow along the waves.*
> *May I spin the flaming wheels of change*
> *And never be trapped within them*
> *Still, amidst endless movement.*

Lakshmi, goddess of wealth; Patta painting from Orissa.

A Hymn to Lakshmi

Lakshmi who heralds victory.

Adi Shankaracharya, the great Vedanta scholar and reviver of Hindu philosophy, who lived in India in the 9th century AD, composed the following Sanskrit hymn in praise of the goddess Lakshmi. In these lines, stress is given to Lakshmi's role as consort of Vishnu-Narayana, personification of the Ultimate Divine Principle. Lakshmi is the medium through which God's grace can be obtained. Her form is both aesthetically pleasing and maternally affectionate. Her glances, filled with the power for God, bestow on the devotee divine grace in the form of material gifts. Hence the hymn is known as the *Kanakadhara Stotra*, the hymn that causes a stream (*dhara*) of gold (*kanaka*) to flow into one's life.

Please note: Since English is not a phonetic language, upper case has been used to produce longer and deeper sounds. Thus, '*dhaaraa*' is written as '*dhArA*.' The translations are not transliterations; they merely capture the gist of the lines. Also, there are several inclusions and exclusions in various renderings of this hymn.

shrI kanakadhArA stotram
the hymn that makes gold flow into one's life

aN^gaM hareH puLakabhUShaNamAshrayantI
bh.rN^gAN^ganeva mukulAbharaNaM tamAlam |
aN^gIk.rtAkhilavibhUtirapAN^galIlA
mAN^galyadAstu mama maN^gaLadevatAyAH　　　**(1)**

May I be blessed by the goddess who is enchanted by the dark body of Vishnu
Just like a beetle attracted to the dark Tamala tree in full bloom

mugdhA muhurvidadhatI vadane murAreH
prematrapApraNihitAni gatAgatAni |
mAlA d.rshormadhukarIva mahotpale yA
sA me shriyaM dishatu sAgarasaMbhavAyAH　　　**(2)**

May I be blessed by the lovelorn eyes of the daughter of the ocean
That glances repeatedly towards Vishnu like a bee flitting around a lotus

AmIlitAkShamadhigamya mudA mukundaM
AnandakandamanimeShamananN^gatantram |
AkekarasthitakanInikapakShmanetraM
bhUtyai bhavenmama bhujaN^gashayAN^ganAyAH　**(3)**

May the eyes that are spellbound by the beauty of Vishnu
Fall on me and bestow upon me prosperity and happiness

bAhvantare madhujitaH shritakaustubhe yA
hArAvallva harinIlamayI vibhAti I
kAmapradA bhagavato'pi kaTAkShamAlA
kalyANamAvahatu me kamalAlayAyAH   (4)

May the glances that satisfy even Vishnu, bearer of the wish-fulfilling gem,
Fall upon me and grant me welfare

kAlAmbudALilalitorasi kaiTabhAreH
dhArAdhare sphurati yA taTidaN^ganeva I
mAtussamastajagatAM mahanIyamUrtiH
bhadrANi me dishatu bhArgavanandanAyAH   (5)

May Bhrigu's daughter, mother of the universe, who adorns Vishnus's chest
Like lightening amongst dark clouds, grant me abundance

Lakshmi who bestows courage.

prAptaM padaM prathamataH khalu yatprabhAvAt
mAN^galyabhAji madhumAthini manmathena I
mayyApatettadiha mantharamIkShaNArdhaM
mandAlasaM ca makarAlayakanyakAyAH   (6)

May she look upon me with affection, she who enabled
Cupid to strike the heart of God

vishvAmarendrapadavibhramadAnadakShaM
AnandaheturadhikAM muravidviSho'pi I
IShanniShIdatu mayi kShaNamIkShaNArddhaM
indIvarodarasahodaramindirAyAH   (7)

Her glance bestows kingship upon gods and makes Vishnu ecstatic
May she rest these luck-bestowing eyes on me

iShTA vishiShTamatayo'pi yayA dayArdra
d.rShTyA triviShTapapadaM sulabhaM labhante I
d.rShTiH prah.rShTakamalodaradIptiriShTAM
puShTiM k.rShIShTa mama puShkaraviShTarAyAH (8)

The celestial regions that grant entry after intense penance open doors if she
wills it, may she look upon me with affection

dadyAddayAnupavano draviNAmbudhArAM
asminnaki~ncanavihaN^gashishau viShaNNe I
duShkarmagharmamapanIya cirAya dUraM
nArAyaNapraNayinInayanAmbuvAhaH   (9)

May the breeze of her compassion bring the clouds of prosperity and
pour rain into the barren life of this poor bird and wash away its
accumulated demerits

Lakshmi who gives knowledge.   105

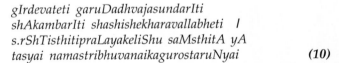

Lakshmi who provides food.

gIrdevateti garuDadhvajasundarIti
shAkambarIti shashishekharavallabheti |
s.rShTisthitipraLayakeliShu saMsthitA yA
tasyai namastribhuvanaikagurostaruNyai   *(10)*

Salutations to the goddess who as fountainhead of knowledge, food and
strength playfully creates, preserves and destroys the three worlds

shrutyai namo'stu shubhakarmaphalaprasUtyai
ratyai namo'stu ramaNIyaguNArNavAyai |
shaktyai namo'stu shatapatraniketanAyai
puShTyai namo'stu puruShottamavallabhAyai   *(11)*

Salutations to the goddess who looks like Aphrodite and sits in a lotus,
consort of Vishnu, who is personification of all wisdom

namo'stu nAlIkanibhAnanAyai
namo'stu dugdhodadhijanmabhUmyai |
namo'stu somAm.rtasodarAyai
namo'stu nArAyaNavallabhAyai   *(12)*

Salutations to the lotus-faced goddess who emerged from the ocean of milk
along with the moon and elixir of immortality to become Narayana's bride

namo'stu hemAmbujapIThikAyai
namo'stu bhUmaNDalanAyikAyai |
namo'stu devAdidayAparAyai
namo'stu shArN^gAyudhavallabhAyai   *(13)*

Salutations to the goddess who sits on the golden lotus, is consort of Vishnu,
is the goddess of earth and compassionate mother of gods

namo'stu devyai bh.rgunandanAyai
namo'stu viShNorurasi sthitAyai |
namo'stu lakShmyai kamalAlayAyai
namo'stu dAmodaravallabhAyai   *(14)*

Salutations to the goddess who is daughter of Bhrigu, beloved of Vishnu
who sits on a lotus and resides on God's chest

namo'stu kAntyai kamalekShaNAyai
namo'stu bhUtyai bhuvanaprasUtyai |
namo'stu devAdibhirarcitAyai
namo'stu nandAtmajavallabhAyai   *(15)*

Salutations to the radiant, lotus-eyed beloved of Krishna,
who is worshipped by the gods as the bestower of worldly riches

sampatkarANi sakalendriyanandanAni
sAmrAjyadAnavibhavAni saroruhAkShi |
tvadvandanAni duritAharaNodyatAni
mAmeva mAtaranishaM kalayantu mAnye   *(16)*

May I always salute you, o goddess who removes all miseries
and bestows peace, prosperity and happiness

yatkaTAkShasamupAsanAvidhiH
sevakasya sakalArthasaMpadaH |
saMtanoti vacanAN^gamAnasaiH
tvAM murArih.rdayeshvarIM bhaje   **(17)**

I salute with thought, word and deed the queen of Vishnu's heart,
whose sidelong glances are carry the promise of wealth
and prosperity

sarasijanilaye sarojahaste
dhavaLatamAMshukagandhamAlyaShobhe |
bhagavati harivallabhe manoj~ne
tribhuvanabhUtikari prasIda mahyam   **(18)**

Seated on a lotus, holding a lotus, anointed with sandal paste,
you gladden my heart, O mother of the three worlds,
beloved of Hari

Lakshmi who grants wealth.

digghastibhiH kanakakuMbhamukhAvas.rShTa
svarvAhinI vimalacArujalAplutAN^gIm |
prAtarnamAmi jagatAM jananImasheSha
lokAdhinAthag.rhiNImam.rtAbdhiputrIm   **(19)**

I prostate before the mother who is bathed each day by the water of the
Ganges, poured from golden pots by white elephants who guard the eight
corners of earth

kamale kamalAkShavallabhe tvaM
karuNApUrataraN^gitairapAN^gaiH |
avalokaya mAmaki~ncanAnAM
prathamaM pAtramak.rtrimaM dayAyAH   **(20)**

Look towards me, O compassionate consort of God, may I, a poor wretch, be
blessed by your divine glances.

devi prasIda jagadIshvari lokamAtaH
kalyAnagAtri kamalekShaNajIvanAthe |
dAridryabhItih.rdayaM sharaNAgataM mAm
Alokaya pratidinaM sadayairapAN^gaiH   **(21)**

With my impoverished heart I surrender myself to your compassion that you
may watch over me, bless me and forgive me

stuvanti ye stutibhiramIbhiranvahaM
trayImayIM tribhuvanamAtaraM ramAm |
guNAdhikA gurutarabhAgyabhAgino
bhavanti te bhuvi budhabhAvitAshayAH   **(22)**

Those who praise the goddess, who is the Veda personified, will be blessed
with good qualities, fame, fortune, and intellect.

|| iti shrImad shaN^karAcAryak.rta
shrI kanakadhArAstotraM saMpUNam ||

This concludes the hymn to Lakshmi composed by Shri Shankaracharya

Lakshmi who grants salvation.   107

108 Names of Lakshmi

To invoke Lakshmi, devotees chant her 108 names that aim to capture the totality of her divine personality. Many of these names are names of the supreme mother-goddess Devi or are shared by other goddesses.

Aditi: feterless; **Ahladajanani**: source of happiness; **Amrutha**: nectar; *Anagha*: sinless; **Anugrahaprada**: responder to pleas; **Ashoka**: dispeller of sorrow; **Bhaskari**: radiant like the sun; **Bhuvaneshwarya**: goddess of the cosmos; **Bilvanilaya**: resides under the Bilva tree; **Brahma-Vishnu-Shivatmika**: companion of the creator, sustainer and destoyer; **Buddhi**: wisdom; **Chanda**: cool like the moon; **Chandrarupa**: Moon-faced; **Chandrasahodari**: sister of the Moon; **Chandravadana**: Moon-faced; **Chaturbhuja**: four-armed; **Daridriyadhwamsini**: destroyer of poverty; **Daridriyanashini**: remover of poverty; **Deepa**: radiant; **Deepta**: flame-like; **Deetya**: answer of prayers; **Devi**: goddess; **Divya**: divine; **Dhanadhanyaki**: bestower of wealth and food grains; **Dhanya**: blessed; **Dharini**: earth; **Dharmanilaya**: residing in dharma; **Harini**: consort of Hari (Vishnu); **Harivallabhi**: beloved of Hari; **Hemamalini**: having golden garlands; **Hiranmayi**: radiant; **Hiranyapraka**: amidst gold; **Indira**: radiant like the Sun; **Indusheetala**: cool like the Moon; **Jaya**: goddess of victory; **Kamakshi**: one with attractive eyes; **Kamala**: lotus; **Kamalasambhava**: emanating from the lotus; **Kantha**: consort of Vishnu; **Karuna**: compassionate; **Lakashokavinashini**: remover of universal agonies; **Lakshmi**: auspicious one; **Lokamatri**: mother of the universe; **Mahakali**: the great devourer; **Mangala**: auspicious; **Narayana Samashrita**: sought refuge in Narayana; **Navadurga**: nine manifestations of the inaccessible one; **NityaPushta**: gaining strength day by day; **Nrupaveshvagathananda**: loves to live in palaces; **Padma**: lotus; **Padmagandhini**: having the fragrance of the lotus; **Padmahasta**: having lotus-like hands; **Padmakshya**: Lotus-eyed; **Padmalaya**: residing on the lotus; **Padmamaladhara**: wearer of lotus garland; **Padmamukhi**: lotus-faced; **Padmanabhapriya**: beloved of Padmanabha; **Padmapriya**: lover of lotus; **Padmasundari**: beautiful like the lotus; **Padmini**: lotus; **Padmodbhava**: one who emerged out of the lotus; **Paramatmika**: omnipresence; **Prabha**: radiant like the Sun; **Prakruti**: nature; **Prasadabhimukhi**: emerging to grant boons; **Prasannakshi**: lively-eyed; **Preeta Pushkarini**: lover of lotus lakes; **Punyagandha**: having divine perfume; **Pushti**: joyful; **Pushti**: possessor of all wealth; **Ramaa**: pleaser of the lord; **Samudratanaya**: beloved daughter of the ocean of milk; **Sarvabhootahitaprada**: granter of universal niceties; **Sarvapadravanivarini**: dispeller of all distresses; **Satya**: totality of truth; **Shanta**: peaceful or calm; **Shiva**: auspicious; **Shivakari**: source of auspicious things; **Shraddha**: devoted; **Shubha**: auspicious; **Shubhaprada**: granter of auspicious things; **Shuchi**: embodiment of purity; **Shuklamalambara**: wearer of white garland and attire; **Siddhi**: ever ready to protect; **Straina Soumya**: showering goodness on women; **Sudha**: nectar; **Suprasanna**: ever cheerful and beaming; **Surabhi**: celestial cow; **Trikalagyanasampanna**: aware of the past, present and future; **Udaranga**: endowed with a beautiful body; **Vachi**: nectar-like speech; **Varalakshmi**: granter of boons; **Vararoha**: ready to offer boons; **Vasudha**: earth; **Vasudharini**: bearer of the burden of earth; **Vasundhara**: daughter of the earth; **Vasuprada**: bestower of wealth; **Vibha**: radiant; **Vibhuti**: wealth; **Vidya**: wisdom; **Vikruti**: multi-faceted nature; **Vimala**: pure; **Vishnupatni**: consort of Vishnu; **Vishnuvakshah**: residing in Vishnu's chest; **Vishwajanani**: mother of the universe; **Yashaswini**: reputed

Lakshmi with her elephants, symbols of nature's power, fertility and abundance; illustration by author.

Select Bibliography

Goddess Lakshmi: Origin and Development; Dr. Upendra Nath Dhal [Eastern Book Linkers]

Devi, Goddesses of India; John Stratton Hawley & Donna Marie Wulff (editors) [Motilal Banarsidass Publishers Private Limited]

Shrimad Bhagvatam; Kamala Subramaniam [Bharatiya Vidya Bhavan]

Puranic Encyclopedia; Vettam Mani [Motilal Banarsidass Publishers Private Limited]

Stories of Lakshmi have been taken from the *Vedas*, *Mahabharata*, *Ramayana*, *Purana*s (especially Bhagavata, Padma, Markandeya, Vishnu and Brahmavaivarta), Lakshmi *Tantra*, Karavira *Shtala Purana*, Tirumala *Sthala Purana*, as well as folk stories that are part of oral tradition and sometimes retold in hymn and prayer booklets.

✳ ✳ ✳

Other Books in the Introduction Series

HINDUISM — An Introduction
Shakunthala Jagannathan

GANESHA — The Auspicious ... The Beginning
Shakunthala Jagannathan, Nanditha Krishna

BALAJI VENKATESHWARA — An Introduction
Nanditha Krishna

SHIVA — An Introduction
Devdutt Pattanaik

VISHNU — An Introduction
Devdutt Pattanaik

DEVI, *The Mother-Goddess* — An Introduction
Devdutt Pattanaik

HANUMAN — An Introduction
Devdutt Pattanaik

110